Nusantara

Indonesia builds a
new capital

First published in the United Kingdom by Bui Jones 2024
Copyright © Robert Templer

Robert Templer has asserted his right under the Copyright, Designs and Patents Act 1988 to be identified as the author of this work

Front cover and map illustration Katie Murphy

buijones.com
Bui Jones Limited Company Number 14823240
Printed and bound in Great Britain by Clays Ltd, Elcograf S.p.A.
A CIP catalogue record for this book is available from the British Library
ISBN 978-1-7394243-5-0 Paperback
ISBN 978-1-0685257-0-4 e book

For Bill and Caroline

Contents

Leaving Jakarta	9
A new capital	17
New capitals	31
Moving the capital	43
Forest city	54
Smart city	63
Splendid isolation	69
Assessing success	77
Learning to love the capital	92
Epilogue	99
Bibliography	103
Acknowledgements	109

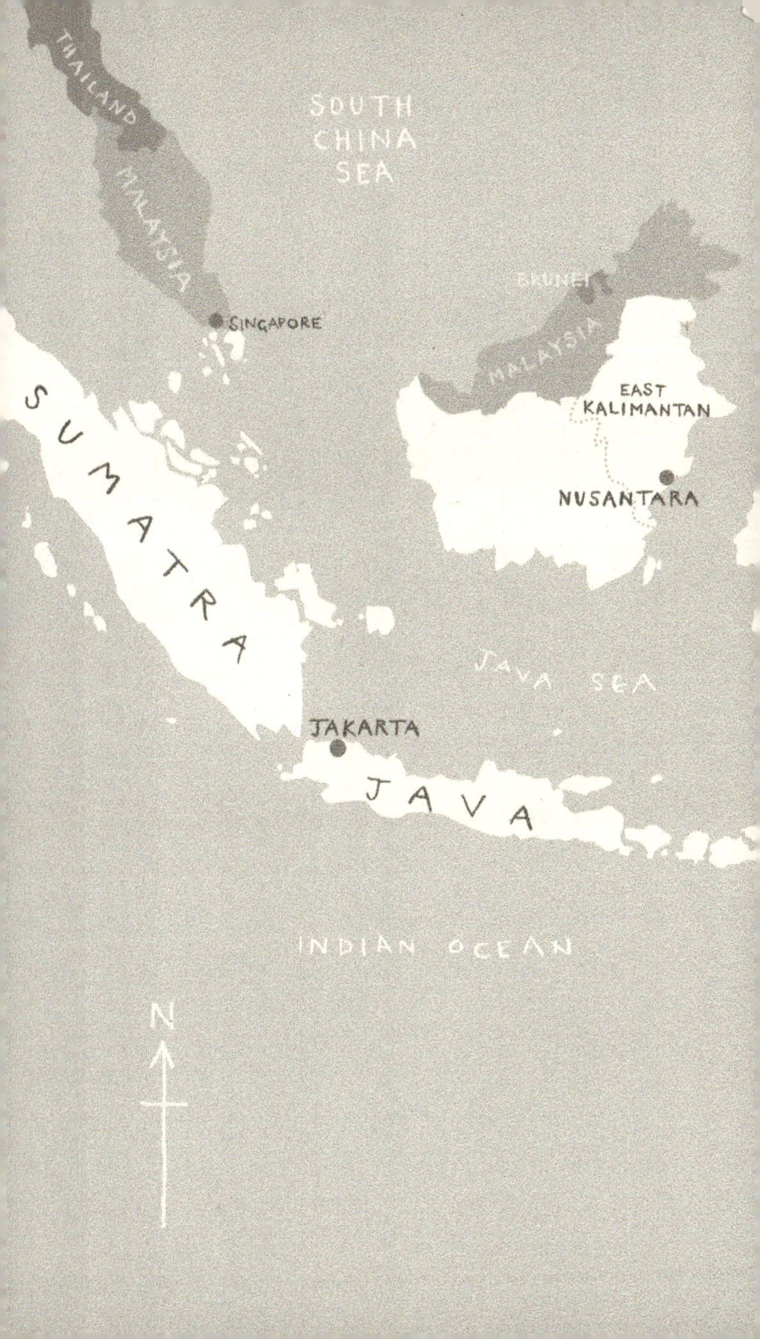
THAILAND
SOUTH CHINA SEA
MALAYSIA
SINGAPORE
BRUNEI
MALAYSIA
EAST KALIMANTAN
NUSANTARA
SUMATRA
JAVA SEA
JAKARTA
JAVA
INDIAN OCEAN
N

Leaving Jakarta

Early on Sunday mornings, before the heat stirs, Jakarta's middle class take to the streets on foot or on bikes, pushing strollers or jogging slowly in small groups. From the Selamat Datang Monument, built by President Sukarno in 1962 ahead of the Asian Games, down to Merdeka Square, the national plaza, the streets are closed to traffic. Families are out early, hoisting up children to be photographed on well-groomed police horses, ears and forelocks covered with fitted white caps and legs spiffed up in striped dressings. Vendors of satay, noodles and Hello Kitty balloons find enthusiastic buyers. Expensive athleisure wear mixes with colourful headscarves and baseball caps. Rival stands advertising mobile services blast K-Pop and a crowd of Girl Scouts passes by in an early start to a lifetime of group outings in matching clothes, an Indonesian national pastime.

This is city life as it should be. Public space devoted to leisure, outdoor activities and fun. By 10 am, the cheerful crowds are gone, and the traffic is back, an unrelenting, roaring torrent of SUVs and motorbikes. Pedestrians now must navigate the exhausting, death-defying video game that is walking in Jakarta. Sidewalks are colonised by mopeds, scooters, barricades, acrobatically parked cars, food vendors, tyre fixers, card players and security booths. What little space remains is a craggy moonscape, often festooned in barbed wire or alarmingly loose electrical cables. At the same time, much of life happens here: food is cooked and eaten, transport negotiated, discussions continue, and the neighbourhood watches.

Jakarta has its charms, mostly hidden in the back streets of quieter neighbourhoods, but it is not an easy city to love. The city has grown at an astounding pace over the past 50 years and hundreds of thousands of people from across the country join the crowded streets each year. A grey miasma has settled over the towers and motorways, resulting from coal-fired power stations built to feed an ever-growing consumer society. Nobody quite knows with much accuracy how many people are in Jakarta. Many commute ever greater distances. Around 11 million live in the city's core, making it only the 30th most populous city in the world. Another 25 million pack into the sprawl of the wider metropolis, meaning it is as populous as Tokyo or Shanghai. Jakarta, by far the largest city in the country of 275 million, has been called the City of a Thousand Dimensions, J-town, and the Big Durian. For its government, it often just seems to be the impossible city.

Jakarta is sinking faster than any other major city, while sea levels are rising at a greater rate than at any time since the end of the last Ice Age. As smog hangs heavily over the city, so does the threat of disaster. Jakarta was built on a large spongy plain crossed by 13 rivers; nearly half of it is below sea level and prone to serious flooding. It has grown without much planning or thought for the movement of its people; private developers threw up vertiginous towers with little consideration of how people would get around. For many years, it was the largest city on the planet without a metro system; in 2019, it finally opened its first line.

When it rains in western Java, as it often does, water runs off hillsides stripped of trees and rushes towards the city. Many of the city's rivers are blocked with debris and have silted up over the years. Housing has been built right up to and even over the edges of rivers—such is the premium on space in crowded *kampongs*. With little green space left to absorb water, there is nowhere for it to go except over the riverbanks and across the city streets. Jakarta is covered with drainage canals and pumping systems that are supposed to control the water. In reality, there is little coordination. One district will dump its water into another without warning. Pumps fail, gates get blocked, and the authorities often neglect to dredge canals. The city government tends to shrug it all off, saying that nobody can control nature. Floods benefit some officials: keeping water levels high prevents informal construction along waterways. This, in turn, opens up land for large private developments built on land raised above the water.

It is mostly the poor who live near waterways, be they natural or manmade, and the poor who suffer the greatest losses. Deaths are now common as walls of water several metres high sweep through neighbourhoods, carrying a deadly cargo of cars, motorbikes and debris. Many more are injured escaping from the filthy black water, filled with human waste and toxic chemicals. In 2020, the worst rains in more than a century caused floods to rise eight metres in a matter of hours. Nearly 70 people died in that disaster.

The media tends to echo government suggestions that floods are an inevitable natural phenomenon and that nobody is responsible. But the reality for many living in the city is the destruction of their homes, sometimes again and again as each inundation hits. The poor lose everything and rarely have the savings to rebuild their lives quickly. Somewhere around half a million people live in *kampongs* along waterways; often, the response to flooding is to evict them from their homes, casting them into enduring penury in the process. To add insult to this injury, they are often blamed for the disasters, accused of blocking canals with their garbage or building too close to rivers.

Floods are not inevitable in Jakarta. As with so many challenges in Indonesia, they result from decades of poor policymaking and a near-complete failure to implement existing rules. The urge to build a modern city of offices and condos only worsened the situation, leading to mass evictions from the *kampongs*. Residents of these areas are rarely rehoused effectively or compensated fairly, nor has the city ever addressed the problem of ensuring that services reach their neighbourhoods.

Jakarta is a patchwork of these informal villages, some of which have been around for centuries, interspersed with modern towers that are sometimes elevated on mega blocks aimed at keeping the city at bay and providing everything residents could need without leaving the building. The effect is often dystopian: towers looming over rough-and-tumble areas where homes are built so close together that there are no visible roads. But these neighbourhoods are vital for the city, becoming home to waves of migrant workers from the countryside, sustaining the economy and providing necessary services to the poor.

Governments have tended to see them as cesspools of crime and the source of so many of the city's problems. But Jakarta is sinking not because of the *kampongs*, but because of the failure to build the hidden infrastructure that is necessary in any city. Subsidence in Jakarta has been evident for at least 30 years, but nothing has been done to tackle it. In 1997, under the influence of the World Bank, Jakarta privatised its water supply, selling the network to British and French firms. Autocrats love their monuments; they never care much about dull sewers or underground water pipes. But as one young Indonesian put it in a despairing tone: 'We will only be a modern country when we can walk on the sidewalks and drink the water.' Both are a distant dream.

Groundwater extraction is supposed to be limited, but it is cheaper and cleaner than piped water, and the rules are not enforced. Much of the city is sinking an average of 15 centimetres a year, with some areas at twice that rate. Pumping of groundwater has led to seawater intruding into the water table, as far as 11 kilometres inland in some cases. Projections are that the city may be at risk of almost total inundation by 2050. Jakarta is not alone in facing the daunting combination of rising seas and sinking land: Bangkok, Dhaka, Shanghai, Guangzhou, Ho Chi Minh City, Kolkata, and Mumbai are all at serious risk.

Jakarta is decades behind other similar cities in addressing the basics. Shanghai, a similar-sized metropolis, started building its metro in 1993 and now has 831 kilometres of lines serving 508 stations. Jakarta started its metro planning three years later and has 13 stations linked by nearly 16 kilometres of track. Traffic in Jakarta defies description; any journey at any time of the day can become a bladder-busting ordeal of many stationary hours.

All of this has come about because of failures in

how the city, indeed the country, has been governed. Since the 19th century, most cities have operated under the idea that providing universal systems—sewers, drainage and water supplies—is necessary to maintain health and order. Jakarta has operated differently. Services are a patchwork of private systems operated for those with power and money. Flooding is now often on a scale that will cost tens of billions to fix, and none of the interventions will be easy. Often the only way for people to protect themselves against repeated devastation is by banding together to raise levees and ensure pumps are present and operational. It is noticeable that ethnic Chinese areas of North Jakarta, where community cohesion has remained strong, have managed to avoid some floods in this way.

Floods in 2007 galvanised the population to action to some degree; not only were they the worst recorded in three centuries, but the head of the city's government was directly elected for the first time that year. Politicians finally had some skin in the game when it came to solving problems. Since then, city governors have deployed increasingly visible efforts to reduce floods. Basuki Tjahaja Purnama, popularly known as Ahok, Jakarta's governor from 2014-17, launched an orange-uniformed army of workers to clear the dams of plastic and other debris that blocked waterways. This persuaded many Jakartans that the government was taking the problem seriously; it also strengthened the false claim that flooding was due to people in poorer neighbourhoods dumping their waste in canals.

Jakarta needs to stop taking water from the ground, and it requires a comprehensive and updated flood management system controlled by a central authority. However, this involves providing piped water and enforcing drilling bans; both are costly and require an effective bureaucracy. Tokyo banned wells in the 1960s when it saw that subsidence was getting worse, slowing its rate of subsidence from 25 centimetres a year to just 1 centimetre—sinking is now no longer a significant problem in the Japanese capital.

Jakarta represents one of the greatest sets of urban challenges anywhere and these are all likely to worsen. The population is both growing and ageing, meaning more people will be vulnerable to heatstroke. By 2050, the number of elderly dying from heatstroke could be 12-15 times higher than the current figure of around 2,000 a month during the hottest times of the year. That is just one of the dozens of problems Jakarta will face as the planet gets hotter, the seas rise and the city sinks. It is no wonder that the government is building a new capital.

A new capital

Seen from high up in the new Presidential Palace, forests stretch to the horizon in every direction, a verdant reminder of how far this is from Jakarta. Below is a ceremonial lawn, a place to welcome state guests to the island of Borneo. Sprinklers sweep across the newly planted grass, already growing strong even as construction continues all around it. Cranes are in constant motion, and workers in hard hats and hi-vis jackets look purposeful. For a massive construction site, relatively little of the land has been ploughed up, and the plantation trees that cover the area, tall and skinny eucalypts, have mostly survived. Despite the ferocious heat, there is an unusual hum of focused energy; deadlines are looming, and the crew are hard at work building Indonesia's new capital.

This is one of the most ambitious projects ever attempted in the country. A budget of US$33 billion is likely to cover just a small part of what is planned to be a large metropolitan area that will eventually be home to four million people. Not only will it replace Jakarta as the seat of government, but the idea is that it will shift economic growth away from the crowded island of Java and rebalance the national economy. This is to be done by developing one of the most forward-looking capitals on the planet, a green and smart city planted with indigenous trees and managed by artificial intelligence.

Nusantara, as the new city has been named, is the latest in a line of new capitals worldwide. They have been built to develop under-populated areas or to escape the legacies of cities established by colonial powers. Some governments have moved their capitals to escape rambunctious politics, ensuring that splendid isolation means there is little chance of a mob storming the palace. Others have tried shifting the balance of power in a divided nation. In most cases, new capitals have become sterile monuments to authoritarian leaders, with boulevards leading nowhere and ministries sitting silent and empty.

Those charged with building Nusantara pledge that this will not happen here. They promise a model 21st-century city powered by renewable energy. Public transport will be built in from the start, as will a circular economy to reduce waste to near zero. Buildings will perch lightly on the ground to allow water and wildlife to move freely. Elevated walkways will connect pedestrians to electric buses; the aim is that people will be able to walk to most services within 15 minutes.

Between the buildings, the jungle will grow again, and land that had been turned into plantations will again support wildlife. Borneo is one of the most biodiverse islands on the planet, home to charismatic fauna such as orangutans, sun bears, proboscis monkeys, flying foxes, clouded leopards, and the world's smallest and most elusive rhinoceros. Protecting the largest of Indonesia's 13,000 islands is vital to reducing the effects of climate change and slowing the inexorable loss of species.* The idea is that Nusantara will lead the way in changing Indonesia's mindset and economy. As a start, a bridge will be built across an expressway to maintain a path used by wild elephants, but the true costs to the environment remain to be seen.

Indonesians know the project as IKN, which is used for both Ibu Kota Negara and Ibu Kota Nusantara ('the nation's capital' and 'Nusantara Capital'), and associate it with President Joko Widodo, known to all by his nickname Jokowi. His fingerprints are all over the project he set in motion in 2019. He chose the location near the southeast coast of Borneo and picked

---

* Indonesia is often said to have more than 17,000 islands, but a count that considered definitions under the United Nations Convention on the Law of the Sea found that the number of islands permanently above sea level was around 13,000. Who knows, really? The figure changes all the time. See Sukendra Martha. The Analysis of Geospatial Information for Validating some Numbers of Islands in Indonesia. *Indonesian Journal of Geography*, Vol 49, No. 2 (2017).

the name, which means archipelago in Javanese and reflects Indonesia's unique and challenging geography. He also selected the designs of some of the most important buildings, likely to become icons for the city and the nation as the government moves over the next two decades and the focus of politics shifts away from Jakarta.

If completed, Nusantara will be a monument to the political skills of a president whose apparently mild manner has belied his success in amassing more power than any leader since Indonesia became a democracy in 1998. Over decades, several presidents have considered a new capital, but Jokowi was the first to move beyond the planning stage. As with most megaprojects in Indonesia, it is fraught with risks. Money tops the list of challenges. Jokowi wants private investment to pay for it, but only some companies, many state-owned, have warmed to the idea. Most new capitals have been money pits, taking decades to complete and never quite living up to their billing. Indonesia, under President Suharto's New Order (1966-1998), tended to rush into grandiose projects, only to lose money or worse. A plan to convert a tract of Kalimantan into paddy fields left a dried-out area of peat fires that smothered Southeast Asia in smoke. A national aircraft project turned out two prototypes with technology from Spain, but never sold a plane. The relocation of millions of people away from the crowded eastern islands, a multi-decade programme known as *transmigrasi,* left many farmers even more impoverished. The Asian financial crisis of 1997 put an end to them all.

Nusantara is an enormous gamble. Jokowi has skillfully made it difficult for any successor to bail on the project. Moving the capital was written into law, and by starting the project with a large presidential complex, any reversal would be embarrassing. He has positioned his son as vice-president, and Jokowi, an energetic sexagenarian, is likely to have a long post-presidency afterlife. Doubtless, Jokowi will be watching carefully to ensure his forest city far from Java does not become a neglected emblem of political overreach.

All new city projects start with a surge of optimism; concept renderings show contented residents amidst mature trees and completed buildings, with no empty lots, construction dust or traffic diversions. The skilled designers of Nusantara have imagined a city of curving and shaded walkways perched on tall columns surrounded by trees. No cars are visible; the electric vehicles allowed in the city will be hidden away from pedestrians. Ministry buildings fringed with plants hide their bulk in the valleys that cross the site while the Presidential Palace rises above them all.

The first stage of the city is being built across nearly 7,000 hectares on the northern side of the site, set away from the coast among low hills. This is a small part of the total area of 256,000 hectares, about four times the area of Jakarta. Here, the government will build the presidential complex, the four coordinating ministries and the first government offices to transfer, including the Ministry of Public Works. More will follow up until 2045, when the capital will be completed in time for the centenary of Indonesia's independence. The area carved out from the province of East Kalimantan will incorporate a full array of functions expected of a city: industries, an airport, a university, and even food production and processing. However, some 70 per cent of the city will be forested, with indigenous saplings replacing the non-native plantation trees growing there now.

The urban plan was inspired by the rainforests that once covered much of Kalimantan. The work of URBAN+, the firm of young designer Sibarani Sofian, was selected from around 300 designs submitted to the government. His idea for a forest city includes ensuring that trees cover the land but also models how forests grow. Tall trees provide a canopy, their leaves gathering energy from the sun. Beneath them, plants wind around their trunks, and animals move through their branches. At the base, their roots bind together the soil, ensuring that rain does not wash it away. In Sofian's design, taller buildings will be topped with solar panels for energy and will provide density so that only 20 per cent of the land surface is built on. Above-ground walkways will connect buildings and allow residents to walk to public transport hubs. They may also be used for deliveries and cabling. The soil, mostly free of concrete and foundations, should reduce the risks of flooding during heavy rains and ensure biodiversity is preserved. It is a design, according to Sofian, 'based on the wisdom of the forests and the culture of Indonesia'.

Nusantara has elements of monumentality that are perhaps necessary in a capital city, particularly that of a large nation with an expanding sense of its place in the world. Drawing on ideas from traditional Javanese cosmology, two axes bisect the site, one running up towards the hills, the other down to Balikpapan Bay and the sea. But these are not avenues for military parades, empty vistas designed to awe the masses or allow soldiers a clear line of sight to shoot protestors. The axis leading up to the Presidential Palace is designed with meandering paths and parks as well as locations for performances. The ministry buildings alongside are set low in the landscape. The Presidential Palace complex is the one truly monumental structure underway, and it is doubtless destined to become a symbol of the city. Part of its vast metal structure is shaped like a Garuda, the bird-god of Hindu mythology that is the national symbol of Indonesia. Its metal wings hug the presidential offices and the palace below, standing above a large ceremonial lawn. It is a unique design that was controversial from the start and is unlike anything built in Indonesia before.

One of Jokowi's most striking decisions was to select a Balinese sculptor rather than an architect to design the presidential complex. Nyoman Nuarta, a sunny, energetic man in his 70s who sports a bowler hat ('Like Charlie Chaplin!', he said), revels in his status as one of the most successful artists in Indonesia. From his extensive museum, workshop and home in Bandung in West Java, he has created works of great diversity: abstract rings of wire bundled into thick metal forms; architectural sculptures that draw on Balinese and Javanese temples; cyclists, horses and even cars caught in motion, defying their tonnage to trail images of speed; and curvaceous women from the Balinese sculptural tradition that pose an erotic challenge to a censorious minority. He has also been the sculptor most associated with national monuments since the 1980s, when he won a competition to immortalise the country's first president and vice-president reading the Proclamation of Independence in 1945.

The past decade has been among Nuarta's most productive. In 2018, he completed a quarter of a century of work on a sculpture of the Hindu god Vishnu riding a Garuda. This enormous work in Garuda Wisnu Kencara Park in Bali is as much architecture as art. It towers 121 metres with a wingspan of 64 metres, making it the size of a 21-storey building and larger than the Statue of Liberty in New York or Christ the Redeemer in Rio de Janeiro.

Initially, there was some opposition to the project; it was enormous; it was said to clash with Balinese beliefs about sacred land; there were concerns about using Hindu imagery to promote tourism, and it was in an area already heavily developed with hotels and tourist facilities. The Bali Post ran a series of articles by cultural figures complaining about its size and location, but comments from most readers were positive. There were many setbacks: fires, death threats, and shortage of funds. It was a massive struggle to build, involving thousands of people. By the time Jokowi inaugurated it, it had become a symbol of pride for both Balinese and Indonesians at large. 'It will not only serve as the icon of Bali's culture and Indonesia's tourism, it will also be a historical footprint of our nation,' the President told the crowds at the opening ceremony.

The statue was finished at a moment when Muslim political groups were challenging Jokowi. His preference has been to keep religion apart from politics in a country where the majority are Muslims but the national ideology officially embraces faith in general and recognises six religions. As the sculpture neared completion, Indonesia was shaken by protests in Jakarta against Ahok, the city's Christian and ethnic Chinese governor. A politician closely linked to Jokowi, Ahok was accused of blasphemy over some remarks he had made about Muslim opponents. Protests organised by Islamist political parties forced him out of office in what appeared to be a resurgence of hard-line religious politics.

It was the most challenging moment in Jokowi's tenure. Nuarta stressed that the statue, inaugurated by the president, dressed in traditional Balinese clothes, was aimed at uniting people under a national banner. 'This statue must belong to the community,' Jokowi said. 'We imported materials from Japan, from Europe, even from Latin America. Then we put them together here, together with artists. The artist is from Bali. The workers are from Bandung, from Java, from Batak, and so on. They were united to complete the GWK ... So, we are truly Indonesian and take pride in it.' This vision of a united Indonesia has held together since the extraordinary nation was assiduously brought into being by its first president, Sukarno, but in any country with hundreds of ethnic groups and more than 700 languages, tensions will always lurk in the shadows.

The large Garuda Wisnu Kencara monument prepared Nuarta and his workshop of many hundreds of workers for their next major project: producing designs for dozens of buildings in Nusantara. For Nuarta, the bird represented protection and was an image that was widely known and accepted by the country's diverse population. Early renderings, however, met with social media comments that the new building was too grandiose, more fitting as the lair of a comic book villain than the office of the president. The design was toned down, and the Garuda was made more enveloping and abstract than threatening. It is made from dimpled sheets of bronze, treated with chemicals and left out in the sun to develop a verdigris patina. Rather than shining as menacingly as it did in those first renderings, its variegated tones make it look soft and hand-made, connecting the building to the traditions of Indonesian handicrafts. The panels were created in Nuarta's sculpture workshop in Bandung and then shipped to the site, where they were mounted on steel frames and inserted into the hilltop structure.

The Garuda will house a series of walkways and bridges linking anterooms and offices and will be filled with trees. It will be a large, leafy atrium, open to the elements, dappled with sunlight, and cooled by the wind blowing through the hills. Its surface will weather further with time, the patina becoming greener and blending with the forests without and within.

Jokowi has set out an ambition to have Nusantara become not just the new capital but a city that is a model for Indonesia and the rest of the world. Government statements have called for the city to host the Olympics in 2036 and to join the ranks of the most liveable cities in the world, a list dominated by cities in Australia and Europe. An unspoken ambition seems to be to replace Singapore as the purported model city of Southeast Asia, from which innovations spread around the region. But Singapore has spent more than half a century quietly promoting quality of life. It over-delivered incrementally on transit, public housing and leisure facilities, steadily upgrading rather than touting utopian futurism. Singapore is a model for a certain type of tightly controlled urban planning that does not always transfer well. The government of the city-state has powers lacking elsewhere and is happy to coerce rather than just nudge people towards certain behaviours. Many Indonesians just roll their eyes at the suggestion that Singaporean discipline could be brought to bear in their country.

The government's ambitious wish list was sent to those who registered for the competition to design the new capital. They wanted a city where 80 per cent of all journeys will be by public transport, about 20 per cent higher than even Singapore. They wanted a zero-carbon city with full recycling of solid waste. It was to be a 'smart city', a rather vague term that generally means the use of sensors to measure everything from traffic flows to alerting authorities when garbage should be collected.

Several cities are being built along these lines around the world, but Bambang Susantono, formerly head of the Nusantara Capital City (or IKN) Authority, charged with the design and construction of Nusantara, wanted something beyond the application of technology. '[We want] a city that is loved,' he told me, mindful of how so many new capitals have turned out to be sterile and soulless. A Berkeley-trained urban planner, Susantono has a boundless enthusiasm for the future city, especially for the idea that it will be populated by happy people. He has even started working with the government of Finland, reputedly the world's happiest country, mostly due to its equality, to find out what creates popular satisfaction. 'My task is to lay a foundation so that friends who are now in their 20s will become owners of the city in the future.' The human factor is at the heart of his sales pitch, particularly to investors. Nusantara may be remote and new, but it will not fall into the trap of so many new cities.

The Authority has bought into every mechanism that might make Nusantara as different from Jakarta as possible. It has a programme to meet the United Nation's Sustainable Development Goals and a committee to oversee its environmental commitments. It is the first city in the country to have a climate change plan. The World Wide Fund for Nature is examining efforts to restore biodiversity and plant indigenous forests. UNICEF has been asked to ensure the city is child-friendly, and the United Nations Population Fund (UNFPA) will examine ways to improve life for women and girls. Plans are afoot for Stanford University to open a Global Sustainability Institute there.

Perhaps most importantly for the enforcement of design guidelines to ensure the city is green and smart is the concentration of power in the hands of the IKN Authority. Ridwan Kamil, a prominent architect who served as mayor of Bandung and governor of West Java, the country's most populous province, is the project's curator, with the power to reject designs or demand changes. 'I tell them "Don't bring Jakarta architecture to IKN … talk to us before you begin the design process",' he said. There was a tendency to want to unleash the glitzy style of what Kamil dismisses as

'Dubai architecture' when the plan calls for buildings that do not just meet environmental standards but integrate plants and trees in their designs. Plans for the city's first hotel were sent back until the building was sufficiently blended into the forest.

New capitals

In our somewhat sour age, with its intractable conflicts and cynical populists, it is hard to imagine the extraordinary optimism of the years when billions of people gained their independence from colonial powers. From 1945 to 1954, Indonesia was among a clutch of nations—Pakistan, India, Sri Lanka, Laos, Cambodia, North and South Vietnam and Burma—that emerged after the shocking turmoil of World War II. None had existed before as modern, independent states within their new borders, and each of them endured profound struggles to establish itself.

Sukarno established Jakarta as the capital in August 1945, when he declared independence. When the Dutch returned the next year, intent on recovering their colony, the new government fled in the night by train, setting up in Yogyakarta. They were followed there by Dutch troops, who took the city in 1948, and captured Sukarno. With their leader exiled to Bangka Island, officials moved the emergency government to Bukit Tinggi on West Sumatra. Indonesia had its third capital in as many years. With the political defeat of the Netherlands, the capital returned to Yogyakarta in 1949 and eventually to Jakarta at the end of that year. Jakarta would be the seat of government for the next 75 years.

In Indonesia, as in many former colonies, the largest city was built under colonial rule as a trading centre to export the country's riches. The new capitals of Karachi, Rangoon, Colombo, and Saigon were all identified by their ports and colonial history. They were also outward-looking, cosmopolitan places, populated by people from all over, throwing off new ideas about culture and politics. That would emerge as a concern for many of the authoritarian leaders trying to assert their singular visions.

Several new capitals were launched on independence. Karachi was one, Saigon another. Laos moved its government from the royal city of Luang Prabang to Vientiane in 1953. Capitals would change with some frequency across Asia: over the next decades, Pakistan, Bangladesh, Myanmar, the Philippines, Sri Lanka and Malaysia would all move or set up new capitals, while almost every other Asian country would at least consider the idea of a fresh start. South Korea and Japan tried to relocate from Seoul and Tokyo, but political obstacles blocked the process. China considered it, as did India.

Pakistan pioneered the purpose-built new capital in Asia, following closely on the heels of Brasília. The country was already a military dictatorship by the late 1950s, and its ruler, General Yahya Khan, was suspicious of the raucous politics in Karachi, home to many of those who had fled India during the Partition in 1947. It was not just a colonial city but also home to a large business community that insisted on having its voice heard. Officially the relocation was about balancing geographical power in the country and moving the government from a vulnerable coastal location. Khan was keen to shift the government to Abbottabad, his birthplace and home of the Pakistan Military Academy, but eventually, a site was chosen just outside Rawalpindi.

Islamabad, a sparkling green and white city with perhaps the most soul-sapping political culture in Asia, was launched in a moment of civic brightness when urban planners and architects still believed in the utopian vision of new cities creating new men. And indeed, this was about men as women rarely featured in those early days of modernism, either as designers or residents of the new cities about which they might have opinions. The new Pakistani capital was designed by a team led by the Greek urban planner Constantinos Doxiadis, who applied all the latest ideas about separating functions into different zones: one for diplomats, one for ministries, one for housing, one for industry, and so on. The low-rise city was laid out below the Margalla Hills in an area known for its bright spring weather and cooling mountain breezes.

Much of Islamabad feels like a luxurious gated community or an expansive retirement village, complete with golf courses, scenic lakes and jogging tracks. Most of its residents, particularly diplomats isolated behind their high walls, are cushioned from the aggressive, even murderous, politics of the place. But it does represent something about Pakistan, being emblematic of the walled-off privilege of the country's military elite, a tiny group that enjoys its own schools, universities, hospitals and access to business sinecures. It is a city of generals awarded large houses on corner plots on retirement, who get to spend their final years far removed from the chaotic, impoverished nation that is their enduring legacy.

Being near Rawalpindi, a short drive down a motorway, has made it convenient for the military to interfere in politics, as it has done constantly since independence. When the violence of Pakistani life creeps into the city, there is always a suspicion that it has happened because someone high up in military intelligence wanted it to happen. This was certainly the case in 1979 when a mob of students from the city's university, organised by a right-wing political party, burned down the US Embassy. General Zia-ul-Haq, at the time a supposed US ally but concerned about upsetting his hard-line religious friends, took 24 hours to send his troops to rescue the Americans trapped in the burning building.

Violence still intrudes into the stillness of

Islamabad; in 2007, radicals took over the Lal Masjid mosque, and the government laid siege for days before soldiers overran it. A truck bomb destroyed a popular hotel in 2008, and a suicide bomber blew up a United Nations office the next year. When conflict does break through into the city, it is part of a performance for the foreigners that live there, a way for the Pakistan military and its intelligence agency to emphasise the vulnerability of foreigners. Both arsonist and firefighter, the Pakistani military has created a capital that is a stage for its national performance of chaos and control.

Brasília was born at a similar time but with a much greater spirit of optimism. Brazil had written into successive constitutions dating back to the 19th century that it would move its capital inland to develop its large, underpopulated interior. President Juscelino Kubitschek had campaigned in 1955 on the slogan '50 years [of progress] in 5' and aimed to deliver profound change to a society marked by its long history of slavery and exploitation. Brasília would reshape the nation, creating a new way of governing, egalitarian and modern in its outlook. To emphasise this, the government chose two architects, Lucio Costa and Oscar Niemeyer, who were idealistic modernists influenced by the thinking of their Franco-Swiss hero, Le Corbusier, the patron saint of utopian urban planners.

As much as Kubitschek was trying to fulfil the national prophesy of colonising the interior of Brazil, he was also eager to leave behind Rio de Janeiro. The city was crowded and divided, too closely connected to a history of colonialism and enslavement. It boiled with contentious politics, such that Kubitschek complained that even a bus strike could develop into the overthrow of a presidency. He envisioned a peaceful capital, modern to a fault but also open, transparent and beautiful. Best of all, it was more than a thousand kilometres from most of the electorate.

A site was chosen in the high tropical savannah. There was no road to get there, so at first, construction materials were flown in by the air force. Costa's city plan signalled what Brasília would be: it was shaped like a plane, the first city of the jet age, the first city where flights were the main link, and a city to be viewed from above. Fittingly, it was built at astonishing speed. Just 41 months after the plan was announced, the capital was inaugurated.

The open plazas, sleek offices and large Superquadra housing complexes represented a utopian future where all classes lived together, inspired by their clean, open surroundings and a new architecture that left behind the country's heavy historical baggage. Reality soon intruded into this vision; no plans had been made to house the thousands of construction workers who flocked from the impoverished north of Brazil. Brasília's first favela sprung up and was quickly named after the president's wife. Niemeyer's monumental and seductive buildings were set far apart, creating not democratic spaces but something like dreamscapes that echoed with notes of isolation, surveillance and control.

Fundamental to the design of Brasília was a fantasy, adopted wholeheartedly by Niemeyer, that Brazil could be an egalitarian society in which, for example, race or class were not divisive issues. His designs subtly drew on many aspects of history, from Baroque churches to the tile work that was part of the Portuguese heritage. But he also projected ideas of equality; the Superquadras were to house a mix of senior civil servants and lowly manual workers, without distinction. Residents were allocated apartments depending on the size of their family. In a country where many middle-class families had a maid, he refused to include staff accommodation in his designs.

The reality was that Brazil was then and remains one of the most unequal societies on the planet, something that could not be wished away by the idealism of the city's designers. Favelas soon sprung up outside the Plano Piloti zone; the Superquadras self-segregated, being taken over by wealthier civil servants; unplanned spaces for shopping, leisure and education all emerged to cater for the large numbers of poor. A city designed for cars failed to accommodate workers, only introducing public transport long after it was needed. Brazilians, however, imposed their own lives on the city, which is now a metropolis of more than three million people that has grown far beyond the design laid out by Costa. From its isolated early days, it is now at the heart of a much more developed agricultural region, connected by roads across the country.

More recently, Kazakhstan and Myanmar have built new capitals, while Malaysia and South Korea have moved some of their government offices to new locations. Their motives have been a mix of politics and planning, burnishing the reputation of a leader and creating an enduring legacy. None of these cities has been an unalloyed success; they remain soulless places dreaded by the bureaucrats required to live there. They all suffer from a deep sense of inauthenticity, architectural 'uncanny valleys' where overly planned cities create an unsettling sensation because they lack any organic urban life.

Putrajaya was built just outside Kuala Lumpur to consolidate the ambitious vision of Prime Minister Mahathir Mohamad. The city removed the government from Kuala Lumpur, a city dominated by ethnic Chinese, who were generally suspicious of Mahathir, as he was of them. The new capital was designed around modernist Islamic forms imported from the Middle East that were to signal a break from the old colonial capital. This was a physical manifestation of Mahathir's desired image for Malaysia: modern, Islamic, efficient, and closer perhaps to the emerging powers of the Middle East than to the West. It was notable how little the architecture, much of it overblown and pompous, referenced Malay culture.

Fittingly, the Prime Minister's Office dominates Putrajaya while the royal families that take turns as heads of state and proved an occasional irritant to Mahathir were left behind in Kuala Lumpur. The tidy new capital, with its oversized offices and expensive landscaping, lacks any sense of place; it is a luxurious suburban office park that could be anywhere. Islamic but modern; isolated from upheavals and political pressures of over-educated urban elites, monumental and hitched to a technological vision of the future that has never appeared, Putrajaya is an expensive warehouse for bureaucrats, most of whom choose to live elsewhere.

Astana, the remote capital of Kazakhstan, took over from Almaty as the seat of government in 1997. The original settlement on the site was known as Akmola, Kazakh for 'White Grave'. It is located far from most of the population, in the middle of the Steppes, in a region known for temperatures that swing between 30 degrees Celcius in the summer and minus-30 in the winter. The oil-rich country splashed out on a grandiose scheme designed by Japanese architect Kisho Kurokawa, one of the founders of the Metabolist Movement and designer of the famous Nakagin Capsule Tower building in Tokyo. The city also ordered designs from 'starchitects' such as Norman Foster. The result is a mishmash of space-age fantasy and semi-Soviet prefab housing set far apart in a landscape of distant horizons and howling winds.

It resembles the site of a post-apocalyptic world's fair; indeed, it hosted Expo 2017. For that, it built a large glass orb resembling the 'Death Star'. This is Dubai architecture, ultimately a cheap and pointless spectacle built in all defiance of the common good.

Building a monument to himself in the middle of nowhere looked like an act of folly by the president, Nursultan Nazarbayev, but was a smart, albeit expensive, political move given the jockeying for power that continued long after the fall of the Soviet Union. The politics behind the city's relocation were complex; clans dominated Kazakhstan, and balancing their power was a key concern. Nazarbayev also wanted to dilute the power of ethnic Russians, a major force in the old capital. The dizzying political dynamics of Kazakhstan are reflected in the fact that the city has had six name changes in six decades. It was briefly named Nur-Sultan after the president left office in 2019, before reverting to Astana, which simply means 'capital'.

Naypyidaw competes with Astana as one of the world's strangest new capitals. Built some 320 kilometres north of the main city of Yangon, it is a town of widely spaced and over-sized monuments, many of them fashioned after images of conquering Burmese monarchs, who often built new capitals as assertions of power. The capital of Myanmar is home to the world's largest parliament, an empty, echoing complex of 31 buildings to represent the number of planes of existence in Theravadan Buddhist cosmology. This garrison capital has special facilities for the military; they chose its location in part because, in their paranoid way of thinking, Yangon was vulnerable to an invasion from the sea. Its wide avenues and sprawling government offices, set far apart in the dusty landscape, create the sense of a fever dream, an idea enhanced by giant, brightly-coloured sculptures. The symbolism in the design and the architecture is all about reinforcing the ethnic Bamar Buddhist elites that dominate the military; there is no room for any expression of the nation's diversity.

Naypyidaw was the vanity project of Than Shwe, a grim parody of a dictator with his sunglasses and medal-encrusted uniforms. He relied heavily on soothsayers and fortune tellers; they decreed that the capital should move on 6 November 2005. Civil servants, given no warning of the move, were ordered onto buses to take them to their new homes in a city covering 4,800 square miles, or four times the area of New York City. It took a month for the junta to reveal the city's name and six months to tell the world that it was the new capital. Officially, a million people are said to live there now, but few believe that figure. The silence of the city is sometimes interrupted by a street sweeper or a lonely car driving along a 20-lane boulevard. Even more than Pyongyang, it is the ideal urban stage for a dictator; perfect order glimpsed through the dark windows of a speeding limousine.

The city was designed to ensure the military could easily take over if they needed to, and on

1 February 2022, they did just that, locking members of parliament into their compounds and closing down the government. While much of the country rose up in fury at the military stepping in again, the empty expanses of Naypyidaw, with its many barracks and population of quiescent civil servants, remained calm. The generals in their citadel could go on looting and killing with impunity.

Moving the capital

Jokowi first publicly broached the subject of moving the capital in April 2019, just a few days after he beat his long-term rival and soon-to-be successor, Prabowo Subianto, to win his second term. Although the president had mused on the subject with journalists and others even before becoming head of state, he did not raise it during the campaign, perhaps knowing that it was not an election-winning idea. In August of that year, during his State of the Nation address, he asked for parliament's permission to begin planning for the new city, which still lacked a location or name.

A new capital was an idea that had surfaced in almost every presidency, going back to that of Jokowi's hero, Sukarno. During the struggle for independence, the capital had shifted around before; in 1950, it landed back in Jakarta. Even under the Dutch, Jakarta was seen as an unfortunate choice for the main city. It was pestilential and flooded often despite a network of canals. In the 1920s, the colonial administration began a move to the more salubrious Bandung, but this was cut short by the Great Depression. Even after independence, it took time to decide if Jakarta, a colonial city dating from the early 17th century, was a suitable location for the government of a new nation.

Sukarno created a committee to study the idea of a new capital in 1947 when he was still waging the struggle for independence. In the late 1950s, he began dreaming of a 'second Moscow' in the heart of the country, an idea encouraged by the new capitals being built in Brazil and Pakistan. A new city would help weave Indonesia together and rebalance development. His friend, the Dayak independence hero Tjilik Riwut, urged him to find a location right in the heart of Indonesia in Central Kalimantan, a province that had been designated for Borneo's indigenous people.

The Dayak general, known for leading the first parachute operation in the history of the Indonesian armed forces, pushed Sukarno towards choosing the village of Pahandut, home to just 900 people living along the banks of the Kayahan River. The village lacked almost any facilities except a derelict airstrip built by the Japanese during their occupation. It was right in the heart of Borneo, the island that was, to Sukarno's chagrin, shared with what would become Malaysia and Brunei. It was also at the geographical centre of the country.

On his first visit in July 1957, Sukarno was not

even able to fly in but took a boat up the river for 36 hours. His visit was a major event for a province that was among the most remote in the country. The village was declared the new capital of Central Kalimantan, and the president laid a foundation stone for Palangka Raya, a combination of Dayak and Sanskrit words meaning 'Great Holy Place'.

The city was to be designed and built with aid from the Soviet Union. Semuan, a friend of Sukarno and a fellow engineer, had been educated in Moscow and received help from Soviet planners in laying out the design. Construction began the year it was declared the provincial capital. Here the history becomes somewhat murky. The grandiose design of Palangka Raya suggests Sukarno may have had ambitions for it to become the new national capital, escaping the colonial legacies of Jakarta, where the government was housed almost entirely in Dutch buildings. But there is little documentation to prove that he wanted to move the capital. It may have simply been a pilot programme to see if Indonesia could build a locally planned city, or it could have been intended as the new centre for Sukarno's short-lived proposal for Maphilindo, a quixotic political grouping of Malaysia, the Philippines and Indonesia. It was a challenging site of marshes and peat that had to be shored up to support foundations. Roads buckled and sank into the soft soil.

Palangka Raya never became the capital but a ghostly memory of its possibilities persists in its broad avenues and roundabouts, built for a ceremonial city of greater importance than the current sleepy town it is. The libraries, theatres, stadiums and grand offices planned in the Soviet style of the time were never built, and the tentative plans to move the capital ended as Sukarno's enthusiasm faded. Building a large city in such a location would be enormously costly. The president also felt that Jakarta had come into its own as 'a historical city, a revolutionary city and an international city', as he said in a 1964 speech to celebrate its 437th anniversary. Later that year, a new law confirmed Jakarta as the capital of Indonesia.

Construction of Palangka Raya stopped in 1967 when Sukarno was ousted and put under house arrest. Tjilik Riwut was removed as governor of Central Kalimantan. The workers building the roads connecting Palangka Raya to the coast of Borneo mostly fled, fearing they would be labelled communists, rounded up and killed.

The idea for a new capital resurfaced under President Suharto in a more modest form. The suggestion was to move the government to Jonggol, not far from Jakarta. Plans for the new city, to be built on 30,000 hectares of a water catchment area not far from Bogor, did not explicitly call it a new capital; it seems the original aim was little more than a new suburb that might eventually house some government offices. It would also be lucrative for the Suharto family and its friends; one study estimated that 80 per cent of the deals involved in building the new city went to cronies. Suharto was forced to step down in 1998. The capital stayed in Jakarta.

The three 'interim' presidents of Indonesia's emergent democracy—BJ Habibie, Abdurrahman Wahid and Megawati Sukarnoputri—lacked the time, money or bandwidth to think about a new capital. The first directly elected leader, Susilo Bambang Yudhoyono, known by his initials SBY, visited Astana, the new Kazakhstan capital, in 2013 and was apparently impressed by its flamboyant space-age modernity. The growing population of Jakarta and some serious flooding convinced him something should be done. His tenure, marked mostly by indecision and passivity, threw up many study groups and commissions but few new policies. One group set up by SBY reported back with the idea that Jakarta remain the capital but money be spent on upgrading its infrastructure. Jonggol could be developed to house some of the government and spread the burden. It also suggested that a new capital should be built eventually but offered few details.

When President Jokowi announced a new capital in 2019 the idea was not met with much enthusiasm. Polls suggested just over half approved of the idea. Support declined when the Covid pandemic became the priority for government and the people alike. Most of those who disagreed with the idea understood the rationale but did not see it as a priority. Even

Jokowi's supporters were somewhat lukewarm. The Javanese strongly backed the plan, even though it meant moving the capital from their home island.

Jokowi pledged to have the first stage of Nusantara open on Independence Day (17 August) in 2024, a tight enough deadline even before the interruption of the Covid pandemic. Given his reputation as the infrastructure president, a sense emerged that he might be the one to get it done. As mayor of the small Central Java city of Solo, he had tackled problems with parks and overcrowding, revived the city's fortunes, and attracted the interest of top political figures in Jakarta. They helped him win the election as governor of the city, where he was most at home opening new markets and chivvying the construction of a high-speed train to Bandung. Jokowi moved fast, harnessing his ability to build coalitions. The law allowing the move to the new capital passed in just 42 days, with only the most perfunctory review by Jokowi's obedient grand coalition and almost none of the detailed studies that would be expected before approving such a massive scheme.

In August 2019, Jokowi announced East Kalimantan as the location of the new capital. It was to be located inland from the eastern coast of Borneo, between the resource boomtown of Balikpapan and the provincial capital of Samarinda. The location was judged to be at little risk from natural disasters, although a study has since warned of landslides causing tsunamis just off the coast. Borneo is mostly free of the earthquakes and volcanos found elsewhere in the Indonesian archipelago. Getting there from Jakarta involves a two-hour flight to Balikpapan and a similar time spent in a car along a winding road choked with construction vehicles. It takes a full working day, although the journey time will be reduced when a major toll road is completed.

The area, which is mostly government-owned, had already been stripped of its old-growth forest and planted with quick-growing trees used for wood pulp. This, along with the low population density, was among the main reasons for the choice of the land, although it has not alleviated all the potential problems. East Kalimantan is crisscrossed with overlapping land-use permits for forestry and mining, as well as historical claims from the local Balik people. Indonesia is riven with land disputes; they occur everywhere, sometimes lead to violence and are notoriously difficult to resolve. Poor maps, boundary challenges, corruption, competing political interests and the low quality of local government all contribute to the problem, which occasionally explodes into conflict. IKN chief Susantono, knowing how closely the local and foreign media are watching the issue, has stressed the fact that few people live in the area currently under development and that they have been brought into discussions about their futures, but human rights groups have warned of potentially explosive tensions given the rushed decision-making over the capital.

Beyond the physical distance, there is a yawning mental gap between Jakarta and a eucalyptus plantation in the dusty red soil of Kalimantan. For many decades, Borneo was the emblematic wild place in Asia, a land of head-hunters, adventurers and criminals on the run, as well as enchantresses that lured men to their doom. The historian Douglas Kammen called it 'Phantasmagorical Kalimantan' to describe how it was portrayed in Western pulp novels and movies from the 1920s onwards. 'An unquiet and mysterious country of inextinguishable desires and fears,' wrote Joseph Conrad in an early novel. As Kammen notes, Borneo is up there with the Amazon, Tibet and the polar regions as places of intense fascination and fear.

Images of the island, the third largest on earth, tend to swing between extremes; it is a place of cataclysmic problems such as wildfires and environmental collapse, with peat fires smouldering across areas larger than many nations and terrified orangutans hounded off their land as rainforests are felled for oil palm plantations. The other side is the utopian vision now being presented by Jokowi: a cultural and environmental idyll that presents the best of Indonesia wrapped in a high-tech gloss with flying cars and plans to host the Olympics.

Residents of Java are inclined to see Kalimantan as a land of exotic Dayak people living in the impenetrable jungle and wearing feathers in their hair. Memories linger of the eruptions of violence in 1997 when Dayaks and recent arrivals from Madura clashed in West Kalimantan. Stories of decapitations spread, awakening legends of head-hunters and raising fears of the disintegration of Indonesia, an idea that persists despite the durability of the republic to date. Coverage of Dayaks today tends towards slightly patronising news stories about rituals or such events as the 'crowning' of Jokowi with a feathered headdress. Various forms of discrimination, particularly in religious matters due to the recognition of only six faiths, are mostly left undiscussed.*

Much of Indonesian identity is formed in the image of Java, unsurprisingly, given its disproportionate share of the population and economy. Nearly every president has come from the island, and almost every key national event has occurred there. For many Javanese, the rest of Indonesia is almost terra incognita. Two civil servants were overheard on the Jakarta Metro wondering with rising alarm whether skin care treatments would be available in the new capital. But the anxieties go deeper. Many Indonesians living on Java know little of their nation beyond their crowded island with its lush climate and rice terraces; until recently, travel within Indonesia was difficult and expensive. Java drew in people from all

* Under laws related to the national ideology known as Pancasila, Indonesia only recognises Islam, Catholicism, Protestantism, Buddhism, Hinduism and Confucianism. Since 2017 it has been possible to leave the religion line blank on documents such as ID cards or use the phrase *penghayat kepercayaan* 'practitioner of belief'. Many Dayaks, some of whom follow a range of indigenous faiths, do this but can face bureaucratic challenges. Some research has put the number of non-official faiths in the country at 245.

over the country searching for jobs, education and opportunities. Those few from Java who left were often impoverished rural families taking advantage of the *transmigrasi* programme that relocated millions of people away from the densely populated western side of the country. Leaving Java is something done by the poor and desperate. Unless you are going to study or shop in Singapore, that is.

Only a few thousand civil servants, military and police will move in the first months after the capital is formally inaugurated. Some 400,000 civil servants are expected to move by 2040, and eventually, the city will have a planned population of more than 1.5 million. They will work in a modern, pollution-free city with commutes that do not drain away your life like those in Jakarta. The aim is to build a lively city that will eventually form a significant metropolitan zone along with the neighbouring towns of Balikpapan and Samarinda, with a total population of more than four million. Ultimately, moving the government could result in as many as half a million people leaving Jakarta, although part of Jokowi's plan is that the bureaucracy will be streamlined and some of its work done by new technology. This number will not make much of a dent in the demands on city services in Jakarta; around 200,000 new residents arrive each year, looking to make their way in the world.

Perhaps the most pertinent and common criticism of Nusantara is that building a new capital does nothing to fix Jakarta's problems. The number of civil servants who will move will not alleviate the relentlessly rising demand for services or transport, nor will it stop the floods. But it will mean that tens of billions of dollars are not available to fix the city, which will remain the most important economic, cultural and social hub. It is rather like the plans billionaires make to settle on Mars: expensive, elitist and of little help to the majority of people. Officials respond by saying that Jakarta will not be forgotten, but it is unclear if Indonesian leaders have the capacity or political will to tackle the city's immense problems.

Forest city

The design for Nusantara draws on the rainforest for its inspiration. At the top of the canopy are those trees that take energy from the sun. Below them are plants that can survive on less light and often form connections through the forest. The ground is soft, a sponge that absorbs water and nutrients, and below it are roots that support and nurture the whole ecosystem. The design envisages tall buildings topped with solar panels but built on columns that preserve the forest and soil below. Raised walkways will connect the buildings, allowing residents to move easily to work, shops or transport hubs when they need to go further afield. Stands of forest thread through the buildings, allowing water to flow and animals to move through their habitats unimpeded. Cars will have limited access; public transport will be considered from the start. Buildings will be surrounded by greenery and in many cases covered with it, softening the edges of the modern office buildings needed to house the government.

Renderings of the designs by URBAN+ offer a slightly otherworldly vision of a city. It is populated by people enjoying the parks and elevated walkways. Everyone looks purposeful and happy, as people always do in architectural renderings or models. Nobody lurks. Nobody sits around engaged in some menial task that barely fills the day or hardly brings in an income. Nobody is busy with the difficult parking of an SUV on a crowded sidewalk or squeezing a moped into an impossibly narrow slot. No bored security guards are shooing people away or vendors blocking the pavements. It appears that Indonesians might be forced to walk hundreds of metres through Nusantara without a single snacking opportunity or the chance to purchase children's clothing, plastic sandals or other necessities. In short, it does not look like anywhere else in Indonesia.

This is certainly a feature of the design of the central government area, but the city is being developed around transport hubs and walkable areas that will have everything needed for a normal life. These will be arranged like small *kampongs* set apart in the forest but linked by walkways and roads. The urban planner Sofian has said that some of the ideas in the design, particularly placing buildings on pillars to spare the ground and create a 'sponge city', draw on traditions of Indonesian architecture without producing folkloric simulacra of Dayak longhouses or Papuan rice barns. The designs have mostly avoided the temptations of either an excess of traditional rooflines or replicating global Islamic modernism's glitzy and awkward decorations, as seen in Dubai or Putrajaya. Some of the more extravagant designs, such as the large presidential office and palace, have been balanced out by more sedate housing, all shrouded in greenery.

Nusantara's design slogan was 'locally integrated, globally connected, universally inspired'. But there is, unsurprisingly, a tension here between what the authorities would like and a design that tries to focus on the human needs of a city. Much is made of inclusion, but the new authority set up to run the city will sit directly under the president, who will appoint the de facto mayor. This may iron out some of the problems that come with elections and could streamline administration, but it will also mean there is no accountability, and residents will have no capacity to shape their city or community. Already, concerns have emerged about the relocation of those living on the site, although the numbers are small, and the government has said it wishes to incorporate them into urban life by helping with training and business opportunities. Administrative capitals often suffer from a democracy deficit, the most notable example being Washington, DC, which elects a non-voting member of Congress and has suffered from decades of poor governance. This lack of participation reflects how Jokowi's interest in democracy declined as he realised how challenging it was to govern Indonesia.

Nusantara is perhaps the most ambitious green city being built anywhere. Many have been launched in the past two decades, but surprisingly few have been completed, and none have achieved the ambitions laid out in their initial plans. Most prominent is Masdar City, designed by the British architects Foster + Partners for a site outside Abu Dhabi. The project, launched in 2006, combined lessons from traditional Middle Eastern architecture with the latest technology to produce a model city supposedly ready for export worldwide. The United Arab Emirates, a nation with 10 per cent of the world's proven oil reserves and one of the highest per-capita productions of greenhouse gases, was to emerge at the forefront of urban environmentalism. Narrow, shaded streets were designed to encourage cooling winds; solar panels would top the roofs while water reclamation systems and personal transport pods would occupy an extensive basement.

Masdar City was to house 50,000 people without producing any greenhouse gases or other waste. Parks would thread through the city to bring in cooling breezes and to encourage walking; wind towers modelled on those found across the region would reduce air conditioning needs despite temperatures as high as 47 degrees Celcius; a solar array was to provide energy. By 2025, Masdar City would be home to 1,500 green tech start-ups staffed by 60,000 commuters coming in each day on an extension of the city's metro. It was all to cost US$22 billion.

Parts of the Foster-designed buildings were given over to the Masdar Institute, a centre for the study of urbanism and the environment. By 2019, the institute had moved out and merged with the country's Petroleum Institute. It was replaced by a new research centre focusing on artificial intelligence and security, the latest issue to grab the attention of Abu Dhabi's rulers. Masdar City was always billed as an experiment, and what it revealed were the immense challenges and costs of building new cities around technology and environmental utopianism. The 22-hectare solar field required constant and expensive cleaning as desert dust blocked sunlight from the panels. Putting the panels on rooftops proved a challenge, as accessing them was never easy. The palms and other plants in the parks rapidly died from a lack of water and had to be regularly replaced. Plans to expand the rapid transit system of driverless pods running under the city were abandoned after a pilot programme proved too costly. The environmental goalposts soon started to shift. Reports from the Masdar Institute trotted out all the latest buzzwords: Carbon Capture! Blockchain! Three-D Printing! 5G! They were all little more than empty business slogans. Per-capita carbon production has been steadily rising in the Emirates, probably the most profligate consumer society on earth. Experts on climate change continue to insist that the only way to tackle the global challenge is to stop using oil and coal. That will never be achieved without some sacrifices.

Masdar City has struggled to attract businesses or residents. A large share of the 5,000 people living there are cabin crew working for Etihad, Abu Dhabi's state-owned airline. Completion dates for the six-square-kilometre city moved from 2016 to 2020 to 2030, and now no date is set. Very few companies have set up shop. Nobody knows how much it has all cost so far, but the joke in Abu Dhabi is that Masdar City spent more money on marketing than construction.

Masdar City's Personal Rapid Transit was popular with visiting dignitaries for photo ops. The German Chancellor Angela Merkel, UN Secretary-General Ban Ki-moon and Indian Prime Minister Narendra Modi all went on joy rides. However, the system proved too expensive to expand beyond a single kilometre— around 30 kilometres were initially planned. One of many problems with the pod system was that it ran in the basement—renamed the 'undercroft'—meaning the whole city had to be raised five metres above the ground. As is so often the case, this new technology was expensive. The metro line was never extended to Masdar City. People had no choice but to use their cars, now parked in sprawling lots around the much-diminished project.

Masdar City is not the only eco-city that has not lived up to its billing. In many cases, there was little economic rationale and no businesses or residents eager to put down roots. People in Abu Dhabi probably have the largest environmental footprint of anyone on earth, given their consumption of subsidised fuel, desalinated water and their nation's levels of oil production. Building a small experimental city at a huge cost has not changed any of those problems.

In China, many new city projects have fallen by the wayside due to political and economic shifts. One that has moved ahead is the Sino-Singapore Tianjin Eco-City, just outside the north-eastern city. Plans drawn up in 2008 projected a population of 350,000 by 2020, but fewer than a third of that number had moved there by then. With cheap housing and good schools, it has proved fairly popular with new residents despite feeling isolated from the city 40 kilometres away. It follows most of the patterns of eco-cities; a corporate enclave where the air is cleaner, the water quality better and the prices set for wealthier members of society. The designers settled for much more modest targets than those who came up with the Masdar City plan, reflecting Singapore's expertise in urban management and knowledge of the enormous challenges of enforcement. The city would only source about half its energy from renewables but would improve efficiency through design and construction practices. Much of its water comes from rainfall collection, desalination and wastewater purification. Planning also focused on economic development to ensure residents could find work: the emphasis was on research, animation, pharmaceuticals and tech industries rather than the polluting heavy industries that had dominated the area in the past.

The biggest question that hangs over Masdar City and other eco-cities is not their usefulness as places of innovation, not the warnings they throw up about certain technologies and how they can be introduced effectively, and not their failure to be examples for other developments. It is the basic question of whether environmentalism should be sequestered at great cost in model eco-cities rather than motivating greater efforts to change the wider society. The arid UAE has consistently had the largest per-capita water consumption in the Middle East, more than three times the global average. Residents enjoy cheap cars, bright green golf courses and parks, and the tourism sector is driven by extremes of conspicuous consumption with desert ski slopes and air-conditioned malls the size of small cities. The UAE is second only to Qatar in per capita energy consumption and third behind two Gulf neighbours in overall consumption of resources. The Gulf States are probably the least sustainable societies on the planet and given that temperatures in the region will only rise, this situation is only likely to worsen.

Environmental concerns have been little more than a marketing gimmick in many of the recent planned cities in India and China, almost all of which involve appropriating farmland and developing properties on it. Almost none of them involve rethinking urbanism with principles such as creating denser cities, building on brownfield sites, shrinking the size of houses, and reducing energy use and consumption. Often there has been little effort to do more than slow the rapid growth in energy consumption in places like Abu Dhabi or China.

It is very difficult to measure the environmental impact of a city. Construction produces an enormous amount of carbon, from the manufacture of concrete and steel and the stirring up of soil to the loss of greenery and the engines of construction equipment. Globally, construction accounts for more than a third of all carbon released into the atmosphere, making it the largest source of warming. The heating and cooling of buildings adds to this. The forest cover and planting in Nusantara should reduce the urban heat island effect, but air conditioning will still be essential. Minimising roads and other areas covered in concrete and shading buildings with solar panels will help reduce temperature rises. However, flying back and forth to Jakarta will emit greenhouse gases, and flights will likely be busy, particularly on weekends. Nearly 100 years after Canberra was built, many residents of the torpid Australian capital still rush to the airport on Friday evenings. Nusantara will likely never truly be a net-zero city when its total energy use is taken into account.

Smart city

The idea of smart cities has been around for decades but nobody is really certain what it means. For many, it involves using sensors and connectivity to manage issues such as energy use, water supply, traffic, waste and security, but how these might be set up and managed varies enormously. Technology can deliver reduced running costs by turning off lights or air conditioning in areas that are unoccupied. It can also monitor waste flows, reduce crime, track transport use or alert city authorities to emerging problems. As AI becomes part of more systems, data collection can be used to provide autonomous management of services, responding rapidly to changing demands. But few smart applications have broken through various barriers to improve the lives of residents in tangible ways; bills go on rising, potholes go unfixed, and municipal websites sit out of service for months.

Most large cities are already smart to some degree. Almost all have a traffic control system or manage garbage collection or road maintenance more effectively. In new developments, Singapore models wind and light patterns to ensure breezes cool buildings and public spaces are shaded from the sun. In public housing, sensors monitor lift movements to ensure they are running; if not, technicians are dispatched automatically. From the start, however, there have been concerns about how smart systems engage with the human realities of cities. In the early days of smartphones, several cities began using an app that would detect potholes and send the locations to local authorities to allow them to be fixed more rapidly. The problem was that at that time, it was mostly the prosperous who owned smartphones, and so more reports came in from richer neighbourhoods. The gap between rich and poor simply widened further. Studies in US cities show that apps that allow people to report problems are most frequently used by wealthier white women with children. All data is skewed in some way.

The promise of the 'Internet of Things', in which everything from water meters to refrigerators are all connected by 5G mobile, appears overstated. City life, particularly in Indonesia, has been changed by ubiquitous delivery services and transport apps, but none of these have emerged through smart city programmes. The language of smart cities is that of major tech firms and consultancies; it seldom works to include the voices of people in city government or to improve the lives of the poor and marginalised. While any tech system can be said to make a city smart, to make a real difference in urban challenges, it should improve access to services, particularly among underserved groups, make governance and service delivery more efficient and help with the greatest challenge of our time, climate change. So far, none of the systems, mostly developed by the usual tech behemoths and consulting firms, have shown that they can deliver much.

Smart cities run into problems over how data is used. Surveillance does not make for a relaxed urban environment and technology can undermine human experiences. A new chain of coffee shops in Singapore only allows you to purchase a drink using their app, which of course, wants to suck up vast amounts of data about your life so the company can sell your data and sell you more. The app does not solve any problems. Smart city tech often has a similar quality of technology desperately searching for a *raison d'etre*. We are already heavily surveilled by our smartphones, and while most people are willing to tolerate that intrusion in exchange for convenience, many failed smart city projects around the world suggest there are limits to how much people want to be watched. A scheme launched by a subsidiary of Alphabet, owner of Google, planned to develop a lakeside district of Toronto as a smart city, but the plan met with growing opposition when it became clear how much data the company wished to vacuum up for unclear uses. It even outlined plans to limit access to those people who refused to hand over their data.

Generative AI tools may be useful in laying out planning options for consultations with citizens and such software can help with modelling the impact of the environment on developments. However, visions of a near-constant monitoring of the behaviour, politics, and desires of city residents quickly become sinister or intrusive. When you crave pizza, do you really want to be nudged towards a healthier food delivery order? Is electronic voting convenient or a mechanism for the authorities to monitor your choices? Do you want more data about your life to be sold to corporations so they can sell you more things you probably don't need? Smart cities tend to be presented as a solution to problems without really identifying the problems. There is a risk that 'smart city' will be little more than an empty slogan and a lucrative business opportunity for the many consultants who promote the concept.

China leads the world in smart city projects, with around 750 approved by 2019. Some of these projects, such as those installing broadband connections, offer widespread benefits, but most seem more like a collusion between the state and tech companies to finesse social control. Increasingly sophisticated surveillance systems now categorise people depending on their behaviour, denying them access to transport and other services if they are deemed 'anti-social'. Ethnic minorities can supposedly be identified by facial recognition; these systems have been used to assert the absolute power of the Chinese Communist Party in such actions as their genocide of the Uyghurs.

Bringing AI in to run city services moves the issue from automation to autonomy; it might be the system and not people deciding how to route traffic, when to pick up garbage or who should have the police called on them. It might decide to lock you inside your autonomous vehicle or drive you directly to a police station if it decides you look or act like a criminal. The technology is available to do all this, and it might come together in a workable system more quickly than we expect, particularly as urban automation is becoming a significant business. An autonomous city brain would control a whole range of aspects of life without necessarily being supervised; indeed, it would likely operate with a quantity of data and at such high speed that it could not be effectively monitored, or even understood. The system could have limits built in along the lines of 'Don't kill the humans', but it would be very difficult to know why it had made certain decisions. One of the problems here is a lack of accountability: in a democracy, city officials are supposed to be able to explain why your planning application has been rejected or why your garbage has not been collected for days.

Indonesia has a long way to go before it needs to worry about autonomous city brains running rampage: there are many pavements, potholes and deadly pedestrian crossings to fix, never mind reducing the pollution that kills or sickens hundreds of thousands. However, some of this technology may arrive rapidly and without much debate, given the general lack of public consultation on Nusantara. The fate of those people who live in the large area planned for development is likely to be a good indicator of the standards of governance that will prevail. We do not know to what extent a capital's security demands will result in ubiquitous cameras and sensors in smart Nusantara. The decline in the quality of democracy in Indonesia and the lack of real oversight in the new capital make this a worrying prospect. An isolated capital already works against political opposition; a web of high-tech surveillance would create an even more isolated and politically sterile ambience.

Splendid isolation

Under Jokowi's presidency, Indonesia finally began to improve its shabby infrastructure, opening up much of the country and improving the prospects for economic growth. This always comes at a cost. Jokowi soon realised after his stunning election victory in 2014 that to get anything done, he could not afford to make enemies of the powerful oligarchs, the military or the political dynasties. The president-elect, Prabowo Subianto, hails from all three groups. Jokowi brought his former rival into government as minister of defence and then gave him a leg up in the February 2024 elections. Jokowi's modus operandi is quintessentially Indonesian. Everyone who needs a slice of the pie gets one, and that way, they do not feel any need to get in the way.

This politicking at least served a purpose. Jokowi clearly had a vision for Indonesia, one that involved developing vast areas outside densely populated Java. In 2014, the president defied public opinion and cut gasoline subsidies, which had mostly benefited middle-class car owners. He then reallocated the $US15 billions saved yearly to improve roads, ports, and airports. 'Indonesia needs national-scope economic justice. There are 17,000 islands, not just one. We need equality and equitable development,' he said at a conference in October 2022. 'This is what we expect from the construction of the IKN.'

The cost of Nusantara has been put at around US$33 billion, with private investors expected to pony up 80 per cent of that, although by March 2024, only a few projects, mostly hotels and hospitals, had attracted private investment. Tax breaks for investment are generous, and it is unlikely that the government will allow investments to fail, but money will unlikely flow in before the city looks like it is going to flourish. That could take some time.

Widening the reach of the economy is certainly a key motive for moving the capital, as is the parlous state of Jakarta. But it is hard to avoid a sense that other issues are at play. Authoritarian rulers have often moved their capitals away from the madding crowds, aware that proximity to dissent represents a constant danger. In turn, capital cities that are remote from the population tend to lead to a decline in the quality of government as rulers become aware that they can steal more and provide less if troublemakers are kept at a distance. This is often the shadowy motive that lies beneath all the talk of balancing development and alleviating pressure on the former capital. Egypt's New Administrative Capital, in the desert 50 kilometres from Cairo, is an example of this, but so is benign, leafy Canberra, whose designers spaced the city out to prevent the sort of dynamic street life that might lead to raucous politics. Its persistent somnolence has prompted such characterisation as 'cemetery with lights' or 'six suburbs in search of a city'.

No officials would openly state that Nusantara is being built to isolate Indonesians from their leaders but this will certainly be the effect. Jakarta, like most long-standing capitals, has the turbulence of history inscribed in its streets. Names do not just conjure locations but also places of political dissent or state repression. Tanjung Priok is not just Jakarta's port but the place where soldiers shot hundreds of demonstrators in September 1984. Trisakti University is not just a private college but also where Brimob (Mobile Brigade Corp) officers shot and killed students in 1998. The streets of Jakarta are the location of the key events that led to the fall of Suharto as well as the violence that followed.

Jokowi was the first president not to come from the country's elites. He was an unknown business owner who became mayor of the Javanese city of Solo before moving from there to Jakarta, winning the election as governor. Two years later, he was president of the republic. He is a slight, apparently unassuming man with no intellectual pretensions, who, in the words of one long-term observer of the country, 'is now as powerful as Suharto [was]'. Although he came up through the parties of Sukarno and Sukarno's daughter Megawati, he seems to admire Suharto's New Order more than the policies of his supposed inspiration. Suharto loved to give advice to farmers—the silent general was often pictured out in a paddy field, perhaps mindful of the old Javanese adage that the success of the rice crops is a measure of a successful monarch. Jokowi prefers the hard hat and the hi-vis vest; he has become, if anything, the image of a powerful mayor of Indonesia, overseeing the construction of new markets, ports and roads. His vision for the country is essentially 'If you build it, they will come'. Infrastructure will open the door to development.

Jokowi has said he wants the new capital to rebalance economic development, a noble intention but one probably not best achieved by moving civil servants to an isolated location. Capital cities in authoritarian countries tend to grow—one study showed they were, on average, 45 per cent larger than capitals in democracies. Indonesia is a good example of this. Jakarta grew most rapidly under Suharto, when economic decisions were concentrated in a few hands. Any successful business had to be near the centre of power, particularly those involved in extractive industries, which have driven economic growth. When success depends on access to licences, business booms in the capital.

Running his furniture company, Jokowi chafed

under this regulatory regime. As mayor of Solo and later governor of Jakarta, he saw civil servants as obstacles and tried to streamline procedures. 'We need an engine with strong power, which is efficient, which doesn't waste fuel, which doesn't get hot quickly, doesn't overheat easily, speeds, but stays cool,' he told civil servants in 2023. At least in part, Nusantara is about creating a leaner, more efficient government in which only dynamic young civil servants will make the move from Jakarta. According to the plan, the new government, working with big data and AI, will become as smart as the new capital itself, clearing the way for development away from the hidebound and corrupt old capital. It has been the dream of many builders of new capitals: a new city will create a new mentality.

It is hard, however, to avoid the conclusion that Jokowi's decision is another step in the process of limiting democracy in Indonesia in the name of creating a more effective, technocratic state. Although there is evidence the idea of a new capital had wormed its way into his thinking quite early in his political career, it did not become a concrete plan until after he had been confronted by an Islamist crowd protesting against his protégé and successor as governor of Jakarta, Ahok, and by the protests organised after the 2019 election by his then-opponent Prabowo Subianto. Eight people died in riots after the former general and now president-elect claimed the election was rigged.

Earlier, on 2 December 2016, around three-quarters

of a million people gathered in Merdeka Square in Central Jakarta. The rally was a follow-up to enormous protests demanding the removal of the city governor. Ahok is an ethnic Chinese Christian politician accused by hard-line Muslims of blasphemy because of a remark he made about his opponents, using a verse of the Koran to turn people against them. This gathering, perhaps the largest religiously motivated crowd ever gathered in the city, followed Ahok's arrest on the disputed charges. Behind the accusation of blasphemy was a surge in resentment of ethnic Chinese and Christian Indonesians, in part stimulated by a rush of investment from China.

Jokowi had skipped the first large protest, leaving it to his vice-president to attend. On December 2, he felt he had to go to diffuse the anger. It was a humiliating moment for the president, who was coming under political pressure to embrace his Islamist opponents and join the mob that had been whipped up against Ahok. The protests signalled a hardening of religious and ethnic divisions and a weakening of the secular nature of national politics. Jokowi's submission to hard-line forces upset his liberal backers, but it was part of a pattern. A president who had risen to power from outside the overlapping circles of oligarchs, military officers and political dynasts soon embraced members of all three groups when he realised he would get nothing done without them.

Since the Ahok protests, Jokowi has seemed to distance himself from Jakarta. He has lived mostly in the presidential palace in Bogor, outside the city. Having to bow to the mob may have set his mind on a transformation of Indonesia's political geography. No Islamist group would be able to muster such a crowd in a new capital in Kalimantan; no mass organisation would be able to wield such power outside Java. Jokowi has been accused of allowing a return to Suhartoism during his time in office, and indeed, as political scientists such as Marcus Mietzner have pointed out, stability has been his priority. Nusantara is likely to add to the gradual anaesthetisation of political life with competition doused, oligarchs and the military returning to the fore and dissent wound in. The harshest critiques come from the old liberals who struggled for much of their careers against Suharto and now see his ghost haunting Jokowi. Goenawan Mohamad, the venerable journalist and founder of the magazine Tempo, was coruscating: 'Jokowi is a traitor, and he betrayed Reformasi.'

The big losers politically of the government's move to Nusantara will be Islamist groups whose power lies in the streets. Jokowi has been careful to keep the two mainstream religious organisations, Nadhlatul Ulama and Muhhamadiya, on his side, but has banned two radical groups—Hizb ut-Tahrir and Front Pembela Islam. After the protests of 2016 shook his presidency—a mob nearly stormed the Presidential Palace in Jakarta, although Jokowi was not there at the time—he drew mainstream groups closer while marginalising hardliners. He widened his coalition elsewhere, moving closer to the military, the police and oligarchs. All of this required some rolling back of democracy, some hardening of the positions of courts and some centralisation of power. As Mietzner writes, this stabilised the presidential system while reducing the quality of democracy, a trend that has been developing worldwide.

Moving the government to Nusantara will temper the power of the street. Not only is Nusantara far away and relatively inaccessible, but also its design mitigates against large crowds in a way that Jakarta's avenues and traffic circles do not. Sukarno's Jakarta was built to impress, but those big civic spaces can also hold many people. Nusantara will be populated almost entirely by civil servants, a natural constituency for those in power, as they depend for their influence on the political leadership. New capitals also lack a history of uprisings to inspire future action; they are places without memories or ghosts.

Politicians will be isolated from constituents. The busy life of daily street protests will continue in Jakarta, barely noticed by the upper echelons of government. If they gather at all, the crowds in Nusantara will likely be sparse and docile. The city will be bare of any history that might remind citizens of any forebears who overthrew their leaders. Nusantara is likely to mute the critical voices of democracy. That works against many people across the political spectrum, from conservative Islamists to progressives; all will find it harder to be heard.

Assessing success

When the Sydney Opera House was being built, it was regarded as a national embarrassment, an extravagant eyesore in a prime site right on the harbour. After the Danish architect Jørn Utzon's design for it was chosen in 1957, almost everything had gone wrong. Not only was its construction massively over-budget, but changes to the design had hampered its functionality. There was insufficient space for scenery and rehearsals, the acoustics were poor, and the orchestra pits were too small. Nine years into the project, Utzon was sacked and left Australia. The building had become a fiasco, the budget soaring from US$4 million to US$55 million. A four-year schedule dragged out to 17.

Utzon never returned to Australia and never saw the finished building. What was often described as a planning disaster became one of the most acclaimed buildings of the 20th century and an icon of its country.

Failure turned into astonishing success. Determining the success or failure of any project is a challenge; it depends on definitions, timing and subjective judgements. Should a new city be measured against the claims made for it on its launch? How much time is needed before a judgment is passed? How will we measure the success of Nusantara? When will it be fair to do so?

We cannot know the future of this new city. Comprehensive assessments can only come with time. But Nusantara already has some awkward echoes with an earlier effort to transform Indonesia through ambitious government programmes. Under the rule of Suharto, his minister for technology and later successor, BJ Habibie, spent billions developing IPTN, an aircraft manufacturer whose signature project was a 70-seat turboprop commuter plane called the N-250. It cost US$650 million to build two prototypes before the project was abandoned due to the 1998 economic crisis. Aircraft manufacturing is an enormously ambitious undertaking. Outside of Europe and North America, only Brazil has developed a successful local industry, but Habibie, a skilled aeronautical engineer, believed his project would vault Indonesia over other countries in Asia and make it a technological power. IPTN drained away government money, even using up nearly $US200 million that had been earmarked for reforestation. Its early success was an illusion; the few foreign-designed planes it assembled were forced on local airlines or sold to the military. The N-250 flew just half the 1,400 hours needed for certification. It never went into commercial production.

Indonesian history is littered with failed megaprojects; there is the ghost of the planned capital at Palangka Raya. Also stretching across this region is the scorched landscape of what was known as the 'Mega Rice Project', a scheme launched in 1996 to turn a million hectares of peat forest into paddy fields. The plan, launched by a presidential decree with little consultation, was a disaster from the start. Peaty soil is unsuitable for growing rice, something the Dayak population could have told the government if it had asked. The region is also prone to drought and fire. The project was one of many planning disasters in the Suharto era when little criticism was tolerated in the media, and few people dared speak up against the fantasies entertained by the president. The area burned in 1997 and again in 2015, releasing astonishing amounts of smoke into the atmosphere. In one year, fires in Borneo were believed to account for around 40 per cent of all carbon entering the atmosphere.

Some decisions about Nusantara are clearly positive. An emphasis on the environment and recreating natural forest cover is welcome, as is the idea of a walkable city with effective public transport, although Indonesia, with its ubiquitous motorcycle taxis, does not have much of a walking culture. Some positive steps are already visible. Extensive housing has been built for construction workers, often an afterthought in these sorts of projects. Some 11,000 workers have been housed in modern quarters with canteens and health clinics, a first in the country. The central government area is being built with a tunnel system for delivering utilities; unlike everywhere else in Indonesia, the city will not be strung with cables, nor will the streets have to be dug up to fix pipes. Water will come from reservoirs and not be pumped out of the ground.

The vision for Nusantara is for it to become a fully-fledged city with all the facilities and sense of place that entails. This will be one of the greatest challenges; cities of government offices tend to have somnolent downtowns after dusk with none of the people or activities that typically animate urban life. The renderings show parks and ceremonial areas, but the city will also have more humanly scaled public spaces, for Indonesia is only really Indonesia with the scents of satay and kreteks on the evening breeze. But what makes for an appealing public space there? To some degree, the public makes public space; areas are colonised informally as people congregate to do whatever they choose: admire and trade caged birds, discuss religion or politics, demand their rights, or often just hang out. The life of a city comes from the bottom up. We have little idea yet how that will turn out.

Nusantara will soon be connected by toll roads to its neighbouring, established cities Balikpapan and Samarinda, both of which have modern airports. Unlike Brasília, Astana or Naypyidaw, it is not being built in isolation but is planned to be the centre of a larger metropolitan area. This means civil servants and others can live in or visit more conventional urban centres if Nusantara proves too sterile and silent for them. It also means that while Nusantara may remain pristine, the neighbours may end up as the dumping grounds for its environmental and social problems. As is often the case, eco-cities simply export their pollution elsewhere. There is also a risk that it becomes not so much a model for urban development but rather something pristine and untouched, set aside just to be admired, like the plastic-wrapped furniture in an unused room kept for guests. Nusantara will only be a real success if the ideas pioneered there become commonplace and the rules that protect the environment and limit the bad behaviour of developers extend across the country.

Perhaps the first judgment will be made on whether Nusantara is even completed. Several new capitals have remained half-built after a government ran out of money or the desire for a move ended with a regime's fall. In Côte d'Ivoire, the capital Yamoussoukro was chosen by President Félix Houphouët-Boigny. It is home to one of the largest churches in the world, the Basilica of Our Lady of Peace, consecrated by Pope John Paul II in 1990. It can accommodate 18,000 worshippers but rarely holds more than 100. The capital remains the seat of government but is a sleepy place that has never lived up to the ambitions set for it by the late dictator.

Yamoussoukro is perhaps not as sad a case as

Gbadolite, the home village of President Mobuto Sese Seko of Zaire, now the Democratic Republic of the Congo. A remote village more than 1,000 kilometres from the capital Kinshasa, it became Mobuto's Versailles, a huge palatial centre that was the de facto seat of government. There were two palaces, one a series of Chinese pagodas modelled on those at the Belgian Royal Palace of Laeken, another a modern building intended only for state functions. There was Africa's only known nuclear bunker and a runway capable of hosting the Concordes Mobuto liked to charter for shopping trips to Paris. Mobuto's palaces were looted when his regime fell in 1997 after 37 years. Soon, the jungle grew back through cracked marble facades.

Jokowi has done what he can to cement his legacy. Nusantara is enshrined in law; this is the first time this has been done for a new capital in Indonesia. To undo it would mean going back to parliament and changing the law, a process that is possible but would be a drain on time and political capital. It would also be embarrassing to abandon the project, as Jokowi actively supported his successor to get him to the presidency and elevated his son to vice-president despite the fact he was below the minimum age specified in the constitution. Prabowo, a former special forces commander with a record of human rights abuses, played on Jokowi's popularity rate of around 80 per cent to win the February 2024 election, presenting himself as a continuity candidate. He and his family will also benefit financially from the city's construction, as do many others who own land there.

Prabowo's continued support, however, is not guaranteed. Jokowi was elevated to the presidency with the support of his predecessor Megawati Sukarnoputri. He soon tired of her interference and steadily distanced himself from her. He also had little truck with the president he replaced, leaving Yudhoyono to drift off into obscurity. Prabowo, who has been hankering to rule Indonesia for decades, is hardly the kind of man to listen to a backseat driver, even if he has pledged to be a continuity ruler. Given his different priorities, it might be tempting to sidle away, crabwise, from the commitment to a new capital.

What could cause delays, or even scupper the new capital, is the state of Indonesia's finances. These generally improved under Jokowi but could still be buffeted, particularly by any sharp downturn in China, Indonesia's largest trading partner. Indonesia only sources around 11 per cent of its GDP from taxes, a third of the average rate in the developed world and around half of those of most of its neighbours. Although Jokowi ended costly fuel subsidies and improved other areas of governance, he also launched a series of very expensive infrastructure and social programmes and has dithered on how open the country should be to foreign investment. Government debt is around 40 per cent of GDP, while the annual budget deficit has been rising. Much focus has been given to the country's exports of nickel, needed for advanced car batteries. Miners are no longer allowed to export unrefined ore, and the government is pushing to keep processing and manufacturing at home to raise revenue. All this comes at a cost; the new eco-capital will likely be funded by burning vast amounts of coal to refine nickel in processes that produce huge amounts of slag and greenhouse gas emissions, all to provide batteries for electric cars.

Prabowo made some considerable spending pledges in his campaign, including free lunches for all schoolchildren, which will cost around US$30 billion over five years. Jokowi managed to maintain the trust of international markets while also pouring money into construction and social schemes. Economic growth had been running at a steady 5 per cent, and although Covid threw a spanner in the works, that was a problem shared by all states. Prabowo will need stable international markets for Indonesian commodities and trusting bankers to pay the bills if he is to maintain popularity with ever-higher spending.

Jokowi and the head of the IKN Authority have worked assiduously to lure investors, but no money has come in from outside Indonesia yet. The MOUs that have been signed have been more aspirational than real—developing flying cars with Hyundai or opening a campus of Stanford University. Local businesses have also hung back, despite all the tax breaks and other incentives.

Another challenge will be maintaining the commitment to environmental standards when the potential investors are the very same entities that have, for decades, profited from corruptly undermining regulations. Environmentalism also means less comfort: hotter homes and offices, walking in the midday heat, and less time in air-conditioned cars. Governments can impose this on civil servants, but investors may be less keen on inflicting such conditions on their demanding customers. It also means higher up-front investment in green construction even if running costs are lower. None of the property behemoths who build projects in Indonesia have shown much inclination towards environmental sensitivity, nor are Indonesian oligarchs known for their commitment to the common good.

Forest Watch Indonesia, Greenpeace and other groups have already criticised Nusantara's performance on the environment, perhaps a little prematurely, although outside scrutiny is a vital aspect of policy-making. Only the most perfunctory studies were done before the choice of location was made, and given that few people live in the area, there is no way to develop inclusive ways to ensure environmental protection ahead of a population moving there. Environmental protection will need the buy-in of civil servants—they will be obliged to swim against the trends by consuming less, walking more, and recycling everything. While the unelected managers of Nusantara may be able to control environmental impacts in the city, they will have no say outside, in the vulnerable forests of Borneo.

Enforcement is a huge weak spot in Indonesia. Environmental codes are in place, but they are almost always ignored. Corruption is so embedded that it forms part of the glue that holds Indonesia together; people simply expect to evade tiresome regulations or get what they need with the help of a bribe or a contact. There is no reason to believe that life in Nusantara will be any different; indeed, given a lack of plans for any sort of democratic governance for the city, it may end up worse. Prabowo has made it clear he favours a return to the New Order approach of his late father-in-law, a time when economic growth always outweighed concerns about human rights or the environment.

Nusantara will be one of several anomalous locations, essentially undemocratic and run by elites in an unaccountable manner. This is not unusual for capitals; they often have arrangements that set them apart from the countries they rule over. Those in favour of minimising participation point to the poor governance of Jakarta and the intrusion of identity politics and religion with the overthrow of a highly competent elected governor, Ahok. The idea that the capital should be a symbol for the nation; a remote collection of elites with only a semblance of democracy and a high-handed view of what is right for people, unfortunately, fits with the political views of the new president.

No major project in Indonesia moves ahead without benefiting the oligarchs who dominate the economy. In some cases, the billionaires who own conglomerates are the only people who can get a project done: they have access to financing, permits, technology and expertise in a way that no smaller business can manage. Most of all, they have political connections. Unsurprisingly, various top property development firms have already found their way to Nusantara, with many already owning land use rights there, originally for mining projects. Both public and private firms have announced plans to take advantage of tax breaks and special rules on land rights. Several Chinese firms, such as CITIC Construction, have said they are interested in projects as their struggles with property markets at home force them to look abroad for opportunities.

Capital cities serve political functions beyond being loveable; indeed, until Nusantara that has never been considered a requirement. Capitals act as synecdoches, a small part of a country that represents the whole. Nusantara will have its giant flag poles, ceremonial lawn, memorials and other spaces for the theatre of state, but to succeed as a capital city, it will need to embody and transmit certain ideas about Indonesia. Jakarta has a handful of public spaces, including those from the colonial period, but is hardly an iconic city. There is no clear urban centre, and it can be hard to distinguish one clump of skyscrapers surrounded by *kampongs* from another. Few buildings or monuments indelibly spell JAKARTA in all caps. The Presidential Palace is a colonial relic, small and subdued. The parliament could be any conference centre, anywhere. The old city of Batavia is a dilapidated colonial relic, although it is being renovated and is popular with local visitors. But Jakarta has history and size. There is no doubt of its importance, expressed in scale and wealth.

Will Indonesians embrace Nusantara? Tourists visiting the site all go to the one existing tourist location, the place where Jokowi launched the project, marked by a small transparent blue cube. A small group of Dayak men and women dance in their elaborate feather costumes. As visitors pose with them, diggers and bulldozers work away in the background. Across Indonesia, there is enthusiasm for the new. The enthusiasm is palpable, but it is not so clear that everyone feels the same way as these visitors. Some of the South Jakarta elite (known as 'Jaksels', a shortening of Jakarta Selatan) have expressed wariness. They have always looked down their noses a little at Jokowi and his provincial ways, but even so, the criticisms have not been noisy, suggesting that they sense a shift in the wider mood in favour of the city. The Jaksels will never be keen on moving, though. Although they cannot evade all the problems of Jakarta, most of them have sufficient wealth to insulate themselves with high-walled gardens, chauffeured SUVs and regular escapes to Singapore. Several generations of the rich and powerful have grown up in Jakarta; their histories, networks, families, and hangouts are all there. Nusantara will be little more than an inconvenience for them.

Some efforts have been made to ensure Indonesians see something of themselves in the new city. The staterooms in the Presidential Palace used for public events have been designed to reflect the diverse cultures of the islands. Jokowi insisted on this after welcoming foreign guests to the presidential palaces in Jakarta and Bogor built by the Dutch. Streets will be named after provinces, and eventually, all the regions of the country will have representative offices in the capital. The six religions recognised by the government will have national mosques, churches or temples there. What may be difficult to capture is a sense of the history of a country whose very existence is something of a miracle.

Nusantara is billed as a major step in rebalancing the economy away from Java. The island has almost certainly exceeded its carrying capacity as far as population and environmental damage are concerned. Unfortunately, resource-based economies in which businesses are dependent on government licences or concessions tend to concentrate in the capital, as they have done in Jakarta. The city will likely remain the focus of finance and resource businesses for some time until power genuinely moves to Nusantara.

The economic impact of Nusantara has been predicted to be fairly negligible, adding just 2.5 per cent to gross domestic product growth up until 2050. The plan involves transferring wealth and human capital mostly from Jakarta to the new city. To generate new wealth, in all its forms, would probably require higher rates of investment than currently planned, to build up the levels of education and health in the new city. There are ways of reducing the Java-centric nature of the economy other than building a new capital. Several smaller new cities might have been built, and some might have even housed ministries or law courts. Educational opportunities could be spread more widely than the universities on Java; Indonesia needs to boost the quality of education and access to it at all levels. Spreading genuine autonomy around the islands would reduce the role of the capital in making business decisions and budgets; one of the reasons Jakarta has grown so large is the enormous concentration of power under Suharto that has partially returned under Jokowi.

Plans to develop East Kalimantan are not without merit but also present risks. Borneo has seen very rapid deforestation, and environmental controls are rarely respected. A new city, even one billed as an eco-city, will likely generate even greater environmental demands. Brasília opened up the interior of Brazil not just for development but for the exploitation of the Amazon, at great cost to the planet. Borneo has the largest peat forests and the largest mangrove forests in the world. They are a vital global resource; their loss will hasten climate change and biodiversity loss to the detriment of everyone. Borneo has 700 unique vertebrate species. It has already suffered terrible environmental harm in recent years. In 2015, an area larger than the US state of Vermont burned. The smoke produced shortened the lives of around 100,000 people across Southeast Asia.

Advocates of eco-cities answer critics by saying that it is necessary to start somewhere and that the world needs models. Proponents of Masdar City argue for the usefulness of experimentation, but the reality is that very few widely adopted new ideas have emerged from that project or any others like it. Nusantara might become a model for urban development in the country as its urban population grows from around 50 to 70 per cent by 2050, if it manages to be economically successful and environmentally friendly as well as socially inclusive, as the IKN Authority head says he wants it to be. This will require a profound change in the way cities develop, with greater efforts by the government to develop low-income housing and less freedom for developers.

But the utopian models that have emerged around the world have not made successful cities. From Masdar City to Songdo, the empty, echoing new suburb of Seoul, technology and the green imperative have not created loveable places. 'There is a tyranny in the womb of every utopia,' wrote the French philosopher Bertrand de Jouvenel. People may long for order, particularly people trying to make sense of an impossible city like Jakarta, but we like it balanced with just enough chaos to feel free.

Learning to love the capital

Indonesians can already take some pride in Nusantara. Their government is building a new capital that lacks much of the ugly bombast of similar projects. Egypt's dictator has built himself a new capital outside Cairo that can only be described as pharaonic. A dystopian vision of skyscrapers and a vast military headquarters in the middle of the desert, it is a sinister fortress designed to resist democracy. It lacks any connection to Egyptian identity in any way, feeling more like the new areas of Shanghai than the capital of a country with one of the world's oldest civilisations. It has cost an estimated US$80 billion, creating a debt trap with China and undermining further the economic welfare of the Egyptian people.

The military government of Abdel Fattah el-Sisi has adopted much of the same rhetoric as Indonesia when it comes to the Egyptian capital; it is to be a smart city aligned with the United Nations Sustainable Development Goals; it is to be a model of new urban development for Egypt and for Africa. However, the enormous new city is predicted to miss these targets by a wide margin, showing how slippery the rhetoric around urban planning can be. It will be an isolated drain on scarce water resources, it provides no housing for the poor, and residents of its expensive American-style suburbs will be entirely dependent on their cars. It is a monstrous, bankrupting vanity project and a cautionary tale for any nation considering a new capital.

The designers of Nusantara often talk of getting people to love the city; those are not words the planners of New Cairo, Putrajaya, Astana or Naypyidaw ever used. While there is a determination to build a city of iconic buildings, something mostly lacking in Jakarta, they are being designed by Indonesian architects in styles that are immediately recognisable as Indonesian. Unlike most cities in the Gulf, Nusantara will not be randomly populated by incoherent baubles from Western 'starchitects' seduced by the limitless budgets of bamboozled sheikhs. The designs revealed to date are diverse; there is none of the modernist uniformity of Brasília's Superquadras, the zaniness of Almaty or the faux-modern Islamic pastiche of Putrajaya, but how they will come together remains to be seen. A strong possibility is that the overall vision could be made coherent by the flow of forests between buildings and the potential lush green beauty of the site. In any case, if the buildings resonate with Indonesians, that is what matters.

The former head of IKN, now charged with raising foreign investment for the project, often quotes a line from Shakespeare's Coriolanus: 'What is the city but the people?' Will Nusantara be able to capture the hearts of Indonesians, particularly in the early years? For a long time, Brasília was the source of many despairing complaints of boredom and loneliness by civil servants who felt banished there. It eventually grew into a city that satisfied the Brazilian soul with its sprawling suburbs and favelas, its country clubs and its churrascarias. Little of the city looks like Costa's master plan, but it does now look like Brazil. Will Nusantara be able to meet its desire to be an eco-city and a smart city without being the sort of soulless, anonymous and often empty development that so many contemporary projects have become? Forest City in Malaysia, Naypyidaw in Myanmar and Songdo outside Seoul are ghostly warnings.

The risk in new cities is that a lack of real history is replaced by a world of dioramas and waxworks, purely official representations of history and identity. The lack of ghosts can translate into a lack of soul, and very little can be done to compensate for that. Art can create some of the dissonance and background hum that animates a place, but the temptation in planned cities is the sort of smooth corporate installations, often surrounded by tinkling water, that only numb the spirit. The human desire for utopian urban order dates back millennia and reoccurs all the time, but is fundamentally misplaced; the spirit of a city only sings when backed by a slightly dissonant and chaotic band.

Nusantara will likely progress in fits and starts, hampered by the inevitable obstacles that surface in Indonesia. Finances will falter, politicians and civil servants will drag their feet, corruption will intrude, and court cases will be drawn out for years. But it will probably get there in the end, its plan compromised and its ambitions trimmed. Will it be a global city, host to the Olympics and a centre for a burgeoning ASEAN? Probably not, given how few purpose-built capitals live up to their very high expectations. Will it be a source of pride for Indonesians? Probably, given that it is the work of Indonesians. They deserve credit for their decision to build a city that reflects real concerns about the environment and the quality of urban life. Could it be an example for urban development in a country in which tens of millions of people are likely to move to cities in the next two decades? Almost certainly not, given the immense challenge of making developers prioritise quality of life and the environment.

For several decades to come, Nusantara will be a fly-in, fly-out capital, a city thinly populated by civil servants and politicians who have left their families back in Jakarta. Nearby Balikpapan, a financial centre for Kalimantan, already has a population that describes themselves as PJKA (Pulang Jumat Kembali Ahad, or 'Home on Friday, Back to Work Sunday').

This may leave Nusantara with a sad divorced-dad vibe: instant noodles in cheap hotel rooms with the briefcase of work open on the desk.

Brasília and Canberra suffered for decades from a similar lack of normal life—few children, a dearth of nightlife and an absence of the vibrant, social, even crazy, manner of their countries' older cities. Due to the potential for economic development in East Kalimantan and the boomtown feel of Balikpapan and Samarinda, the capital may be different if it can harness some of their buzz. Canberra and Brasília were also designed around the motor car, creating mostly soul-sapping emptiness rather than cheerful street life. Nusantara, at least, will be walkable if it sticks to its plans.

Building a new capital is expensive and risky. Adding technological and environmental requirements as a focus of urban life makes it even more so. China's construction boom over the past decade has shown that many risks do not pay off. Self-declared smart cities, such as Songdo in South Korea, have mostly been a bust, as have purpose-built zones for tech industries. Cyberjaya, the Malaysian tech hub built alongside its new capital Putrajaya, never attracted the investment or talent needed for high-tech advancement, in part because it was such a dull place to live. Just as much as technology, successful cities need the arts, museums, and performances, and not just those that come out of worthy national institutions. Nusantara has plans to expand education; universities, research centres, art and music schools would enliven the capital as long as they are free to produce work of genuine interest.

The lesson from the many new cities built worldwide in the last century is that they do not resolve the problems of the societies that built them. Unsurprisingly, as capital cities, they reflect the social and political realities of those nations. Nusantara is likely to do the same. Rather than the global city imagined by Jokowi, it is much more likely to remain a city that exists in isolation, a model perhaps of thoughtful design but unique in a country of traffic-clogged, crowded metropolises. It is also likely to be an outpost of elites with none of the cosmopolitan jumble of Jakarta where all of Indonesia's people, rich and poor, converge. There may be an effort to promote biodiversity in the city, but it will likely be a social and political monoculture consisting of civil servants and their political masters. As their populations change with the rise and fall of governments, it can take decades, some would even say centuries, for purpose-built capitals to build a sense of identity. Brasília now looks less like the future and more like old Brazil with its inequalities, teeming favelas and insecurity. Will Nusantara follow this path with a pristine government area surrounded by the sort of informal *kampongs* common in other Indonesian cities? Achieving the vision laid out for the capital will take unprecedented levels of planning, enforcement and financing.

Indonesia is a huge, diverse country. It looks inwards more than outwards, and so even a capital that is shaped by what are perhaps elitist concerns around sustainability and liveability is still likely to be a success and a source of pride, just as the new high-speed train on Java is proving to be. It will be modern, different from elsewhere and, importantly, designed and built by Indonesians. Those characteristics alone will help win it support. But smoothing the edges of everything in Nusantara would be a shame. It should reflect a diverse sense of the archipelago for which it is named: the Indonesians who seemingly live in different moments in history across the vastness of their country, the Indonesians who struggled for independence and democracy: the Dayaks who lived on its land; the migrants; the artists; the factory workers; the techies; the farmers; and the street vendors. Every Indonesian who visits their capital should see something of themselves there.

Epilogue

Nusantara was due to be inaugurated on 17 August 2024, the day Indonesia celebrates its independence. Jokowi attended events at the new presidential palace along with 1,300 guests but did not issue the presidential decree formally moving the capital from Jakarta. It was no surprise that the project was behind schedule. Not enough housing for civil servants had been completed, and many administrative buildings still needed to be fitted out. Of course, this generated some doubts about the whole enterprise: Was there sufficient funding? Would Jokowi's successor close the project? Would Jokowi's attempt to leave a lasting legacy fail?

Given that the timetable for the city extends out more than 20 years, it may be too soon to make a judgment. The incoming president Prabowo has pledged to continue the project, although he rarely sounds enthusiastic about it. His priorities will likely be his populist school lunch programme and expanding the military, a favoured institution that he feels has been neglected. Economic growth in Indonesia is expected to be a reasonable, if not spectacular, 5 per cent or so for a few years. This would allow for continued steady development of the new capital.

To prosper as a city rather than just survive as an administrative backwater, it will need investment from the private sector and in cultural and educational facilities. Universities and arts hubs are not only sources of economic vibrancy but also create a circulation of people and ideas essential in political cities. A somnolent city of bureaucrats needs the zest of a busy civil society and the noise generated by cultural centres. It will need art and performance, movies and business, architecture and nature. It will need a sense of place.

This is the most difficult aspect of urban design. There have been so many recent failures, perhaps because the tech bro fantasies of the designers of green and smart cities dominate those who know that a city engages all five senses, that it varies across the day, that it requires some bustle and crowding, places where people gather and places where people walk. It requires the city square, the temple garden, the park, the shopping street, and the car park where hawkers set up their stalls at night. There is no app for any of this. New cities cannot create the history that contributes to a sense of place; attempts to do this create a fake Epcot Centre vibe that flattens the past into traditional rooftops and false facades. New cities need new architecture that explores the past and brings it into the present. It needs to embrace older ideas—shaded walkways, tree-lined streets, the capture of breezes, and the cooling effects of water—to address the current problems of climate change and environmental degradation. Creating a place nowadays means addressing the failures of past urbanism—clogged traffic, unwalkable cities, a disdain for nature, an excessive embrace of hierarchy and separation—and coming up with new urban experiences that involve very different engagements with the world.

The most important judgment on Nusantara will not be if it meets somewhat arbitrary deadlines, as predicted from the start it would not. It will be if it is able to create something Indonesian, forward-looking, sustainable, and bold. Something that might just be an example for us all.

Bibliography

Bland, Ben, *Man of Contradictions: Joko Widodo and the Struggle to Remake Indonesia*, Penguin, 2021

Bolleter, Julian, and Cameron, Robert, 'A critical landscape and urban design analysis of Egypt's new Administrative Capital City', *Journal of Landscape Architecture*, Vol.16, No. 1, 2021, pp. 8-19

Bunnell, Tim, et al., 'Points of persuasion: Truth spots in future city development', *Environment and Planning D: Society and Space*, Vol. 40, No. 6, 2022, pp. 1082-1099

Bunnell, Tim, Goh, Daniel P.S., Lai, Chee-Kien, and Pow, C.P., 'Introduction: Global Urban Frontiers? Asian Cities in Theory, Practice and Imagination', *Urban Studies*, Vol. 49, No.13, 2012, pp. 2785-2793

Caljouw, Mark, Nas, Peter J.M., and Pratiwo, 'Flooding in Jakarta: Towards a blue city with improved water management, Bijdragen Tot de Taal-, *Land- En Volkenkunde*, Vol. 161, No. 4, 2005, pp. 454-84

Campante, Filipe R., Do, Quoc-Anh, and Guimaraes, Bernardo, 'Capital Cities, Conflict, and Misgovernance', *American Economic Journal: Applied Economics*, Vol.11, No. 3, 2019, pp. 298-337

Colven, Emma, 'Subterranean infrastructures in a sinking city: the politics of visibility in Jakarta', *Critical Asian Studies*, Vol. 52, No. 3, 2020, pp/ 311-331

Dovey, Kim, Cook, Brian, & Achmadi, Amanda, 'Contested riverscapes in Jakarta: flooding, forced eviction and urban image, *Space and Polity*, Vol. 23, No. 3, 2019, pp. 265-282

Egreteau, Renaud, 'Power, cultural nationalism, and postcolonial public architecture: building a parliament house in post-independence Myanmar', *Commonwealth & Comparative Politics*, Vol. 55, No. 4, 2017, pp. 531-550

Fealy, Greg, 'Bigger than Ahok: Explaining the December 2 Mass Rally', *Indonesia at Melbourne* (blog), The University of Melbourne, 7 December 2016

Gökçe Günel, 'Masdar City 2020', *Middle East Report*, No. 296, Fall 2020

Gökçe Günel, *Spaceship in the Desert: Energy, Climate Change, and Urban Design in Abu Dhabi*, Duke University Press, 2019

I-Chun, Catherine Chang, 'Building Ecopolis in the World's Factory: A Field Note on Sino-Singapore Tianjin Eco-city', in Kreuger, Robert, et al. (eds.), *Adventures in Sustainable Urbanism*, State University of New York Press, 2019

James Holston, *The modernist city: an anthropological critique of Brasília*, University of Chicago Press, 1989

Koch, Natalie, *The Geopolitics of Spectacle: Space, synecdoche, and the new capitals of Asia*, Cornell University Press, 2018

Lamb, Kate, '"Jokowi effect": How Indonesia's outgoing leader shaped election to succeed him', *Reuters*. 12 February 2024 https://www.reuters.com/world/asia-pacific/jokowi-effect-how-indonesias-outgoing-leader-shaped-election-succeed-him-2024-02-12/

Lau, Julia et al, *The Road to Nusantara*. ISEAS Yusuf Ishak Institute, 2023

Lorinc, John, *Dream States: Smart Cities, Technology and the Pursuit of Urban Utopias*, Coach House Books, 2022

Macedo, Joseli & Tran, Levu V., 'Brasília and Putrajaya: using urban morphology to represent identity and power in national capitals', *Journal of Urbanism: International Research on Placemaking and Urban Sustainability*, Vol. 6, No. 2, 2013, pp. 139-159

Marcus Mietzner, *The Coalitions Presidents Make: Presidential Power and Its Limits in Democratic Indonesia*, Cornell University Press, 2023

Martha, Sukendra, 'The Analysis of Geospatial Information for Validating Some Numbers of Islands in Indonesia', *Indonesian Journal of Geography*, Vol. 49, No. 2, 2017

Moser, Sarah, 'Rejecting and Reproducing Colonial Urbanism in Putrajaya', in Hahn, Hazel H. (ed.), *Cross Cultural Exchange and the Colonial Imaginary*, NUS Press, 2019, pp. 187-214

Muhtadi, Burhanuddin, 'Analyzing Public Opinion on Moving Indonesia's Capital: Demographic and Attitudinal Trends', *ISEAS Perspective*, No. 54, 2022

Mujani, Saiful & Liddle, William R., 'Indonesia: Jokowi Sidelines Democracy', *Journal of Democracy*, Vol. 32, No. 4, 2021, pp. 72-86

Myoe, Maung Aung, 'The Road to Naypyitaw: Making Sense of the Myanmar Government's Decision to Move its Capital', *Asia Research Institute Working Paper Series*, No. 79, 2006

Nugroho, Yanuar & Adrianto, Dimas Wisnu, 'The Nusantara Project: Prospects and Challenges', *ISEAS Perspective*, No. 69, 2022.

OECD, 'Revenue Statistics in Asia and the Pacific: Key findings for Indonesia', 2020, https://www.oecd.org/tax/tax-policy/revenue-statistics-asia-and-pacific-indonesia.pdf

Office of Assistant to Deputy Cabinet Secretary for State Documents & Translation, 'President Jokowi: IKN to Provide Equitable Development', Cabinet Secretariat of the Republic of Indonesia, 18 October 2022

Pisani, Elizabeth, *Indonesia, Etc.*, W.W. Norton, 2014

Preecharushh, Dulyapak, *Naypyidaw: The New Capital of Burma*, White Lotus, 2009

Rossman, Vadim, *Capital Cities: Varieties and Patterns of Development and Relocation*, Routledge, 2016

Rykwert, Joseph, *The Seduction of Place: The History and Future of Cities*, Vintage Books, 2002

Scott, Margaret, 'Indonesia's Corrupted Democracy', *New York Review of Books*, 4 April 2024

Shimamura, Takuya & Mizunoya, Takeshi, 'Sustainability Prediction Model for Capital City Relocation in Indonesia Based on Inclusive Wealth and System Dynamics', *Sustainability*, Vol. 12 No. 10, 2020

Stierli, Martino, 'Building No Place: Oscar Niemeyer and the Utopias of Brasília. *Journal of Architectural Education*, Vol. 67, No. 1, 2013, pp. 8-16

Syaban, Alfath Satria Negara & Appiah-Opoku, Seth, 'Building Indonesia's new capital city: an in-depth analysis of prospects and challenges from the current capital city of Jakarta to Kalimantan', *Urban, Planning and Transport Research*, Vol, 11, No.1, 2023

Sze, Julia, *Fantasy Islands: Chinese Dreams and Ecological Fears in an Age of Climate Crisis*, University of California Press, 2015

Varquez, A.C.G., Darmanto, N.S., Honda, Y., et al., 'Future increase in elderly heat-related mortality of a rapidly growing Asian megacity', *Sci Rep*, June 2020

Verheijen, Bart & I. Nyoman Darma Putra, 'Balinese cultural identity and global tourism: the Garuda Wisnu Kencana Cultural Park', *Asian Ethnicity*, Vol. 21, No. 3, 2020

Waschmann, Adrian, *Brasília–an analogy of modernism*, Grin Verlag, 2013

Wu, Pei-Chin, Wei, Meng (Matt), & D'Hondt, Steven, 'Subsidence in Coastal Cities Throughout the World Observed by InSAR', *Geophysical Research Letters*, Vol, 49, No. 7, 2022

Acknowledgements

My thanks go to Minh Bui Jones, for being receptive to the idea of this book, as well as the many people who helped me in Jakarta and in Kalimantan. Many thanks are due to Rin Hindryati, who was an endlessly helpful colleague. Peter Mares, Philip McClellan, Elizabeth Pisani and Jim Della Giacoma all provided helpful comments on drafts. Among those who are owed much gratitude are Greenpeace and Indonesia Forest Watch, as well as: Hasanuddin Zainal Abidin, Deka Anwar, Ben Bland, Bambang Brodjonegoro, Tim Bunnell, Tommy Firman, Sidney Jones, Douglas Kammen, Ridwan Kamil, Julia Lau, Muslim Muin, Cynthia Lakshmi Nuarta, Nyoman Nuarta, Karim Raslan, Jo Santoso, Adam Schwarz, Sibirani Sofian, Achmad Sukarsono and Bambang Susantono.

ROBERT TEMPLER is a writer, lecturer and policy consultant. His latest book, *A Basilisk Glance: Poisoners from Plato to Putin*, was published by Bui Jones. His previous book, *Shadows and Wind: A View of Modern Vietnam*, was published by Penguin.